AF594314

BUDDHAS *of* BURMA

Photography by
Jean-Pierre Grandjean

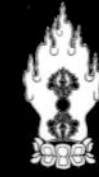

Shambhala
Boston
2002

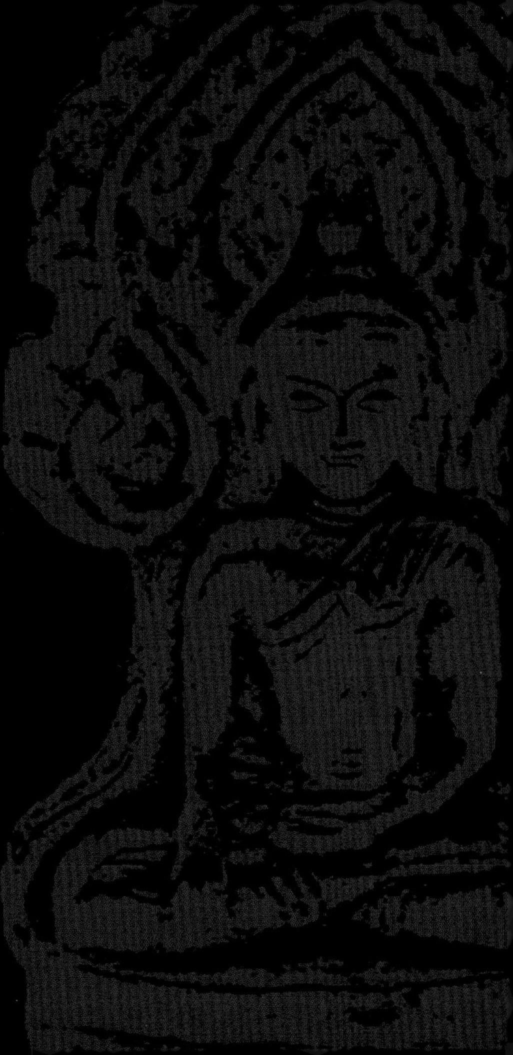

Buddhism has been an integral element of the Burmese culture and national identity for the nearly one thousand years since the great king Anawratha unified much of the country and established Theravada Buddhism as the state religion. Anawratha's reign, which began in 1044 CE, also marked the beginning of Burma's golden age of Buddhist art, centering on the ancient city of Pagan. Over a 250-year period, Anawratha and his successors built several thousand brick temples, stupas, and monasteries on a plain along the Irrawaddy River. This bustling capital and religious center was overrun by Mongols in the late thirteenth century and was nearly abandoned. Yet the remains of roughly nine hundred brick temples, five hundred stupas, and four hundred monasteries still rise above the plain, a reminder of Pagan's former glory.

Despite invasions, colonial occupation, and political strife, Buddhism has continued to exert a powerful influence in Burma (which was renamed Myanmar in 1989). Painted and gilded Buddha images in stone, metal, wood, and clay grace Burma's countless temples and shrines. Monumental sitting, standing, and reclining Buddhas serenely survey the land scape, promising release from suffering. Red- and white-robed monastics are a common sight, with a total of more than 400,000 monks and 75,000 nuns in some 6,000 monasteries across Burma. The monastic community, or sangha, maintains a close, symbiotic relationship with lay Buddhist followers. Laypersons regularly donate food, clothing, and other necessities to the sangha, enabling them to pursue lives of renunciation and spiritual aspiration. In return, lay followers accrue spiritual merit for their generosity and benefit from the example of the sangha, who embody the life and teachings of the Buddha. In this way, the sangha and lay community are able to advance together along the path to enlightenment.

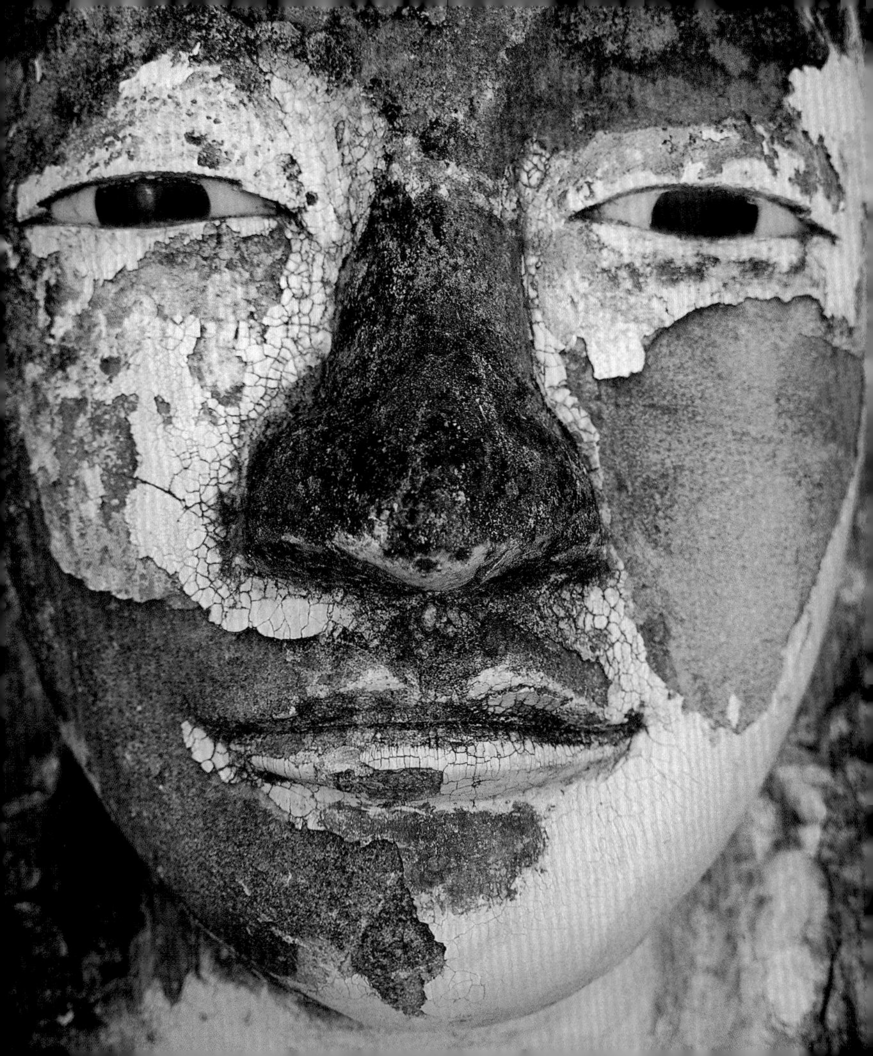

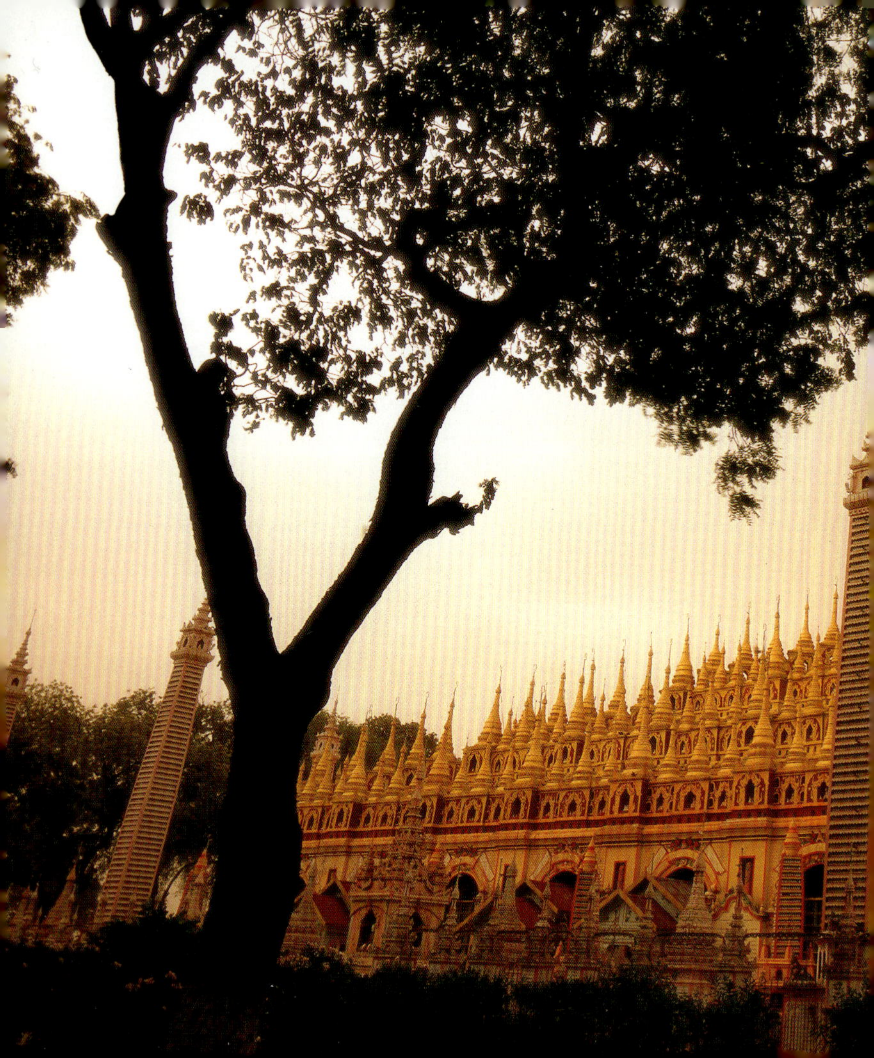

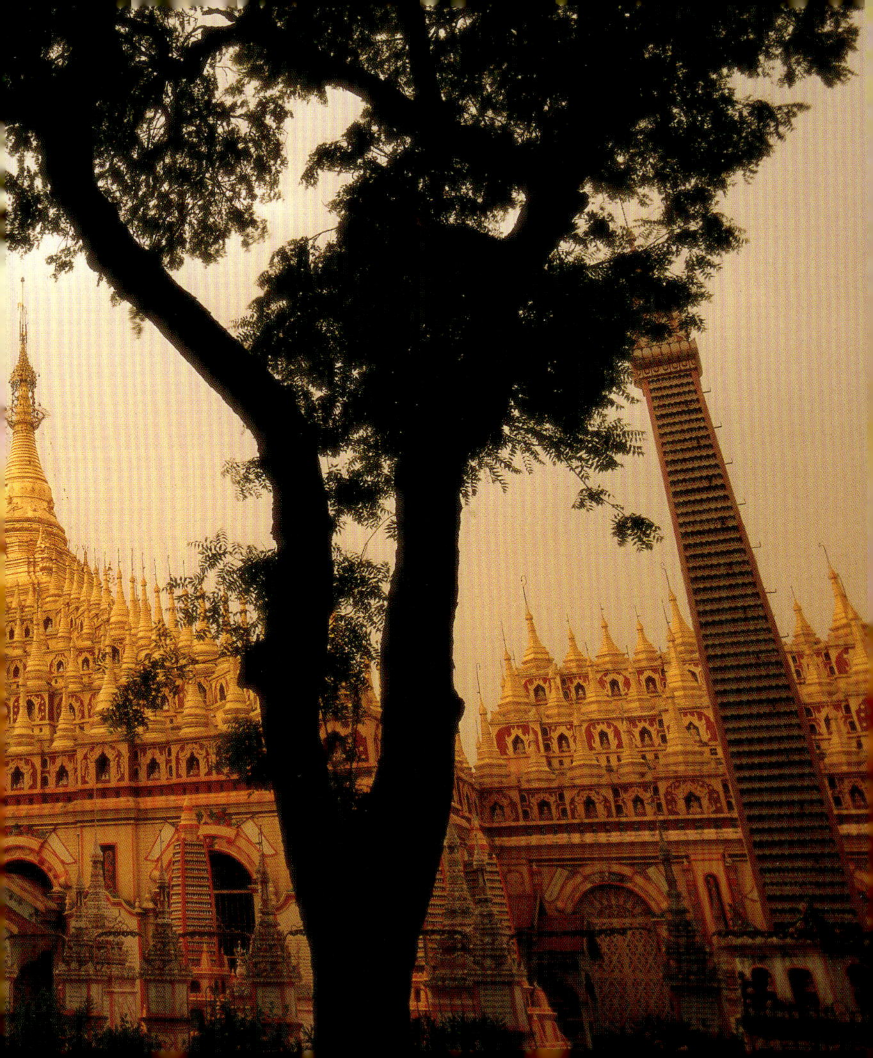

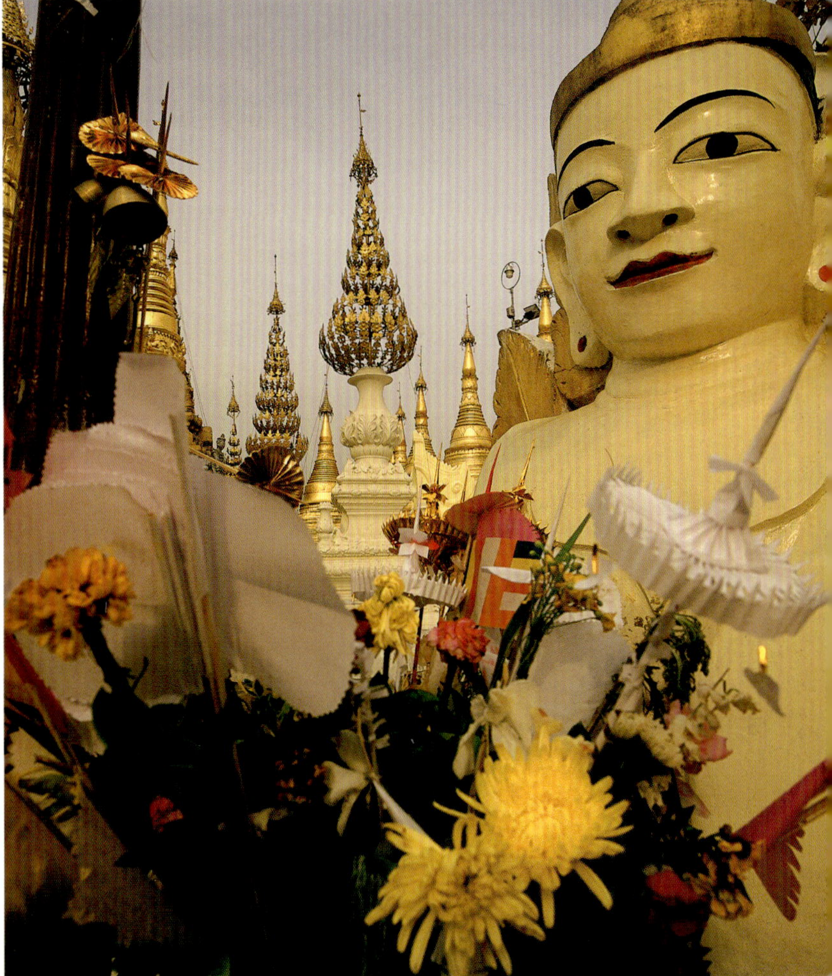

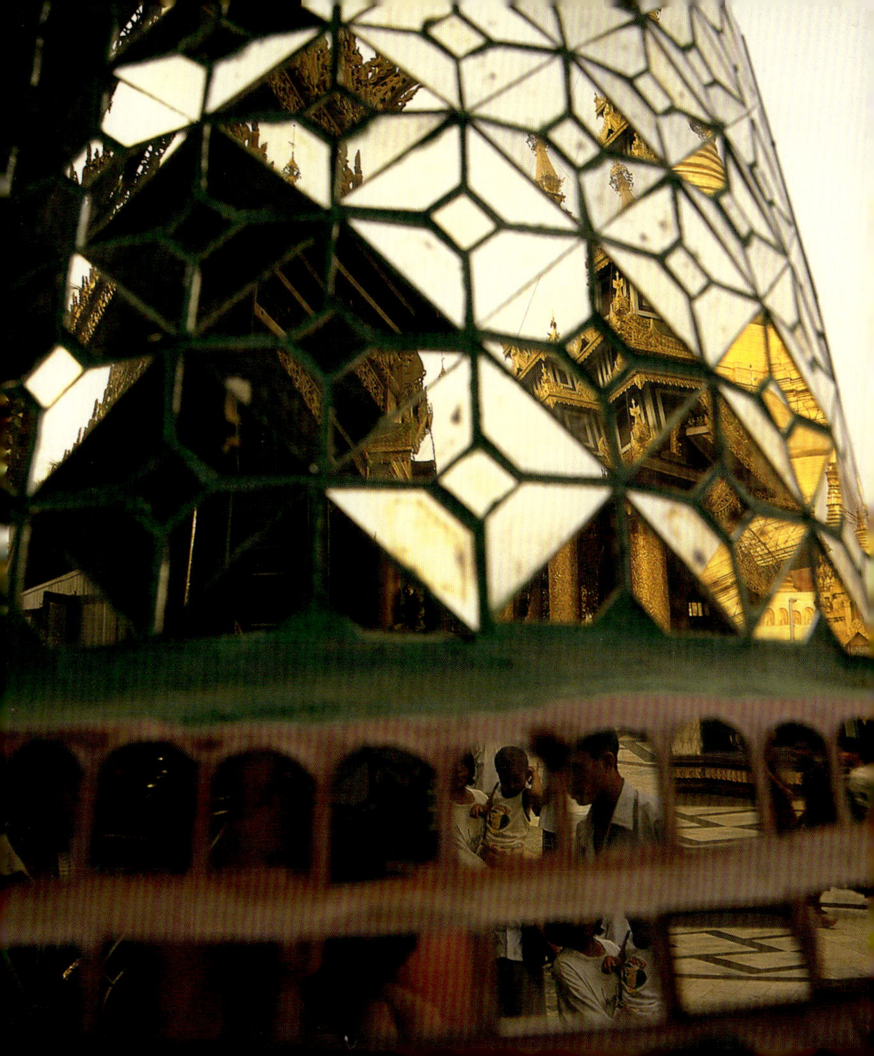

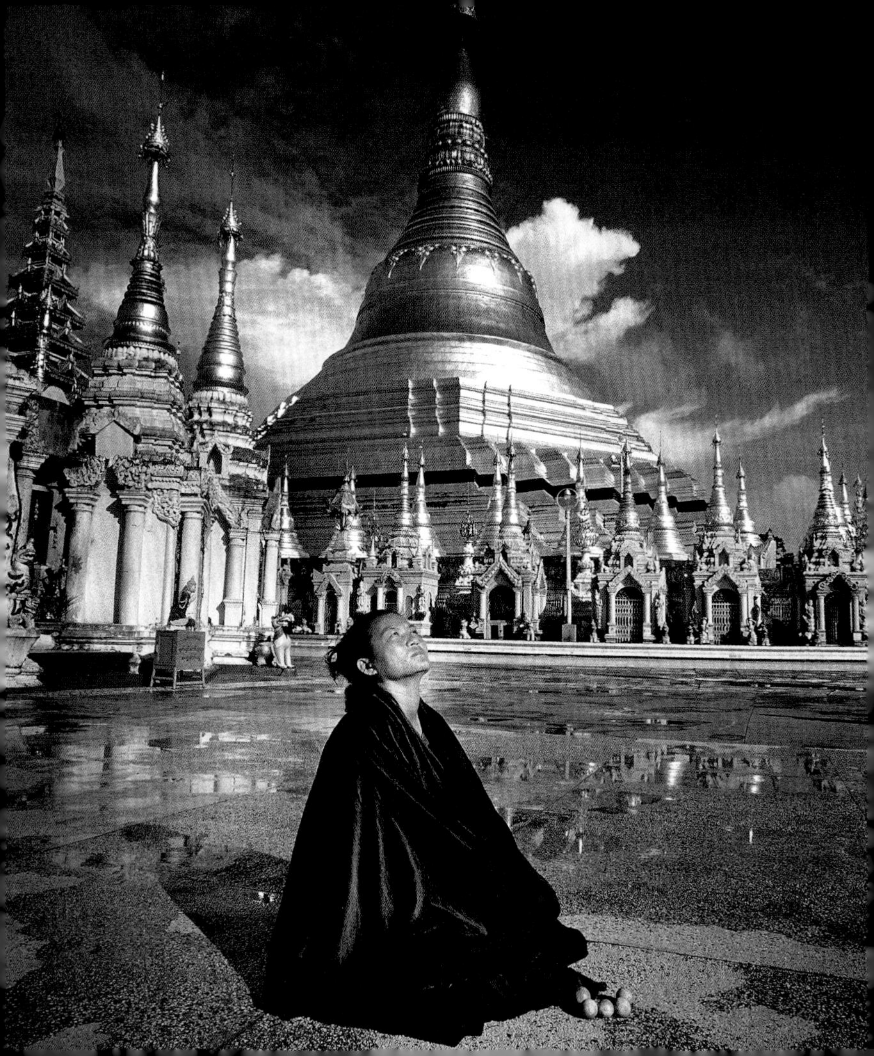

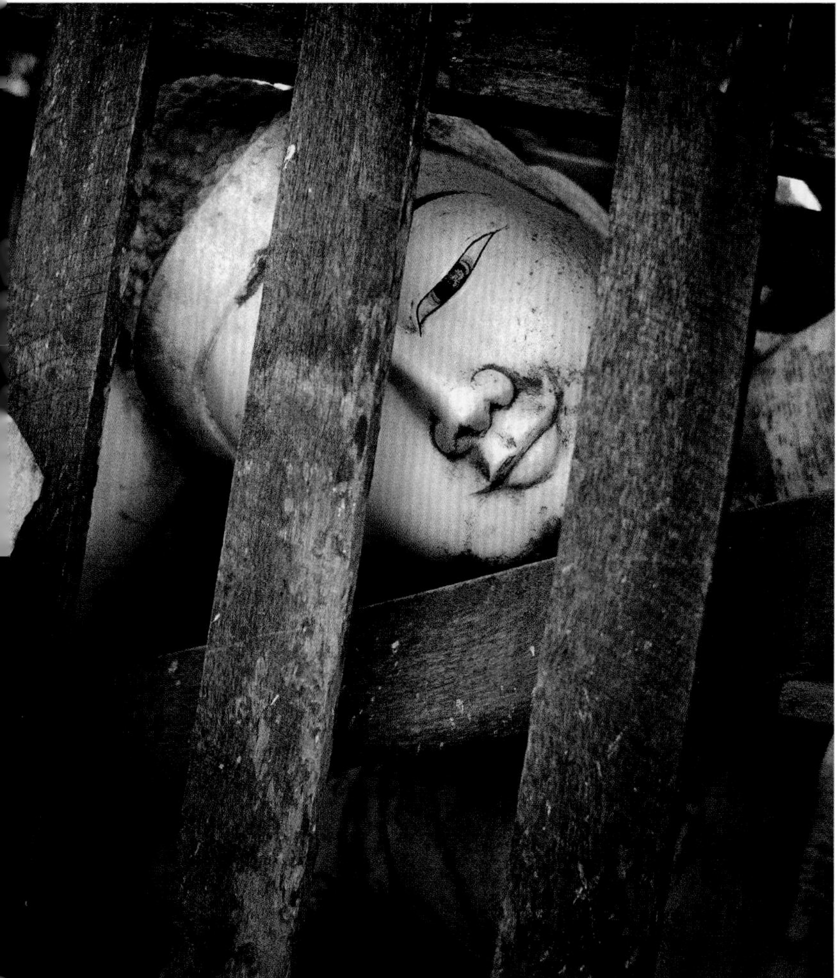

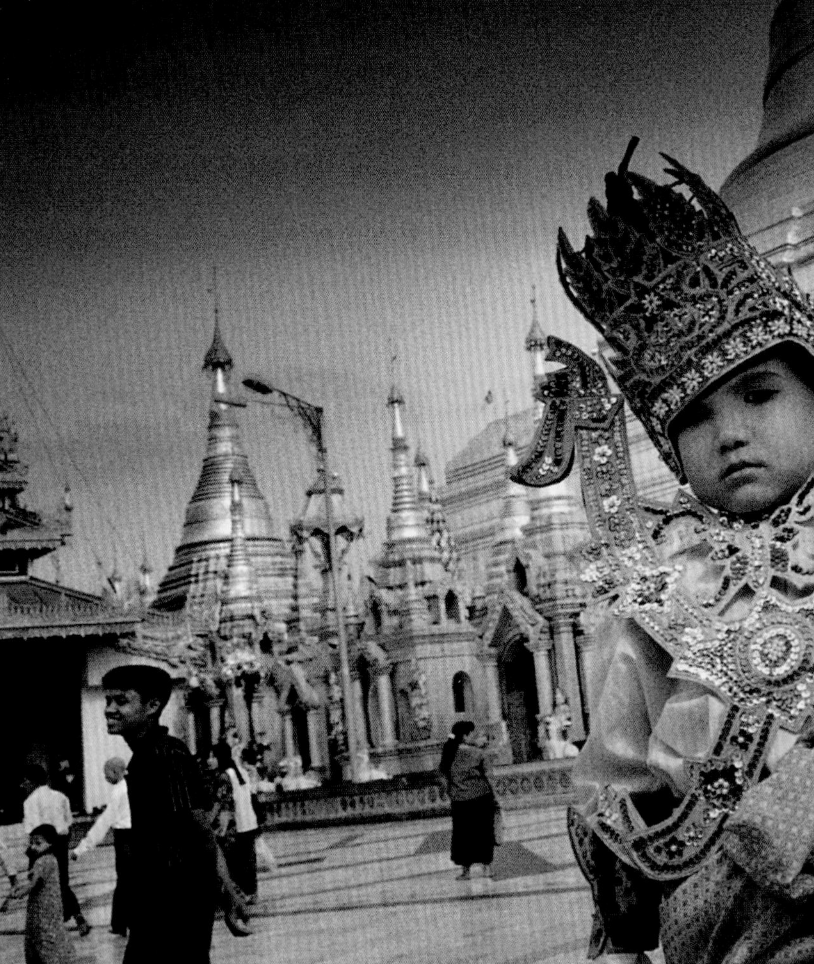

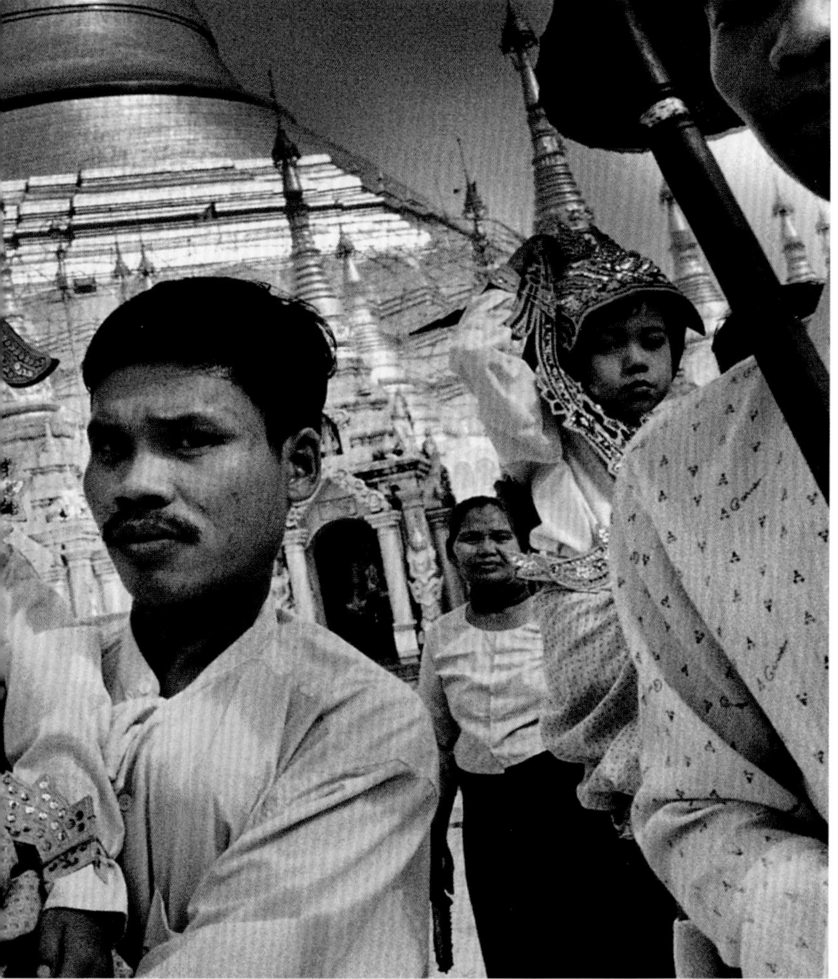

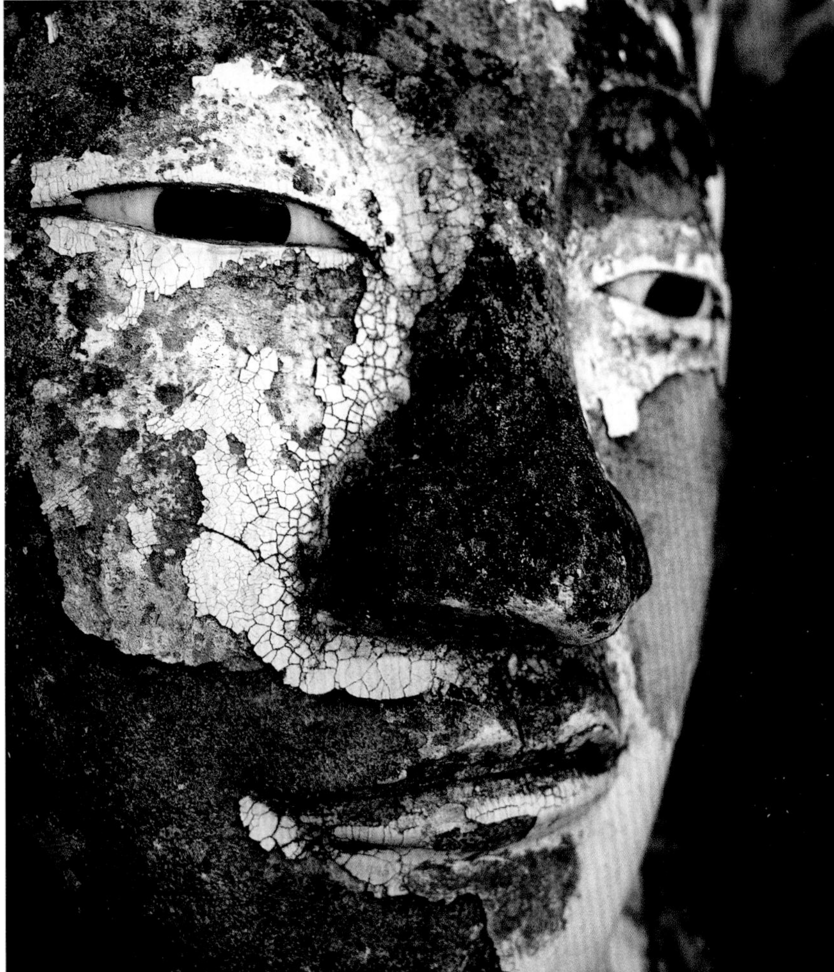

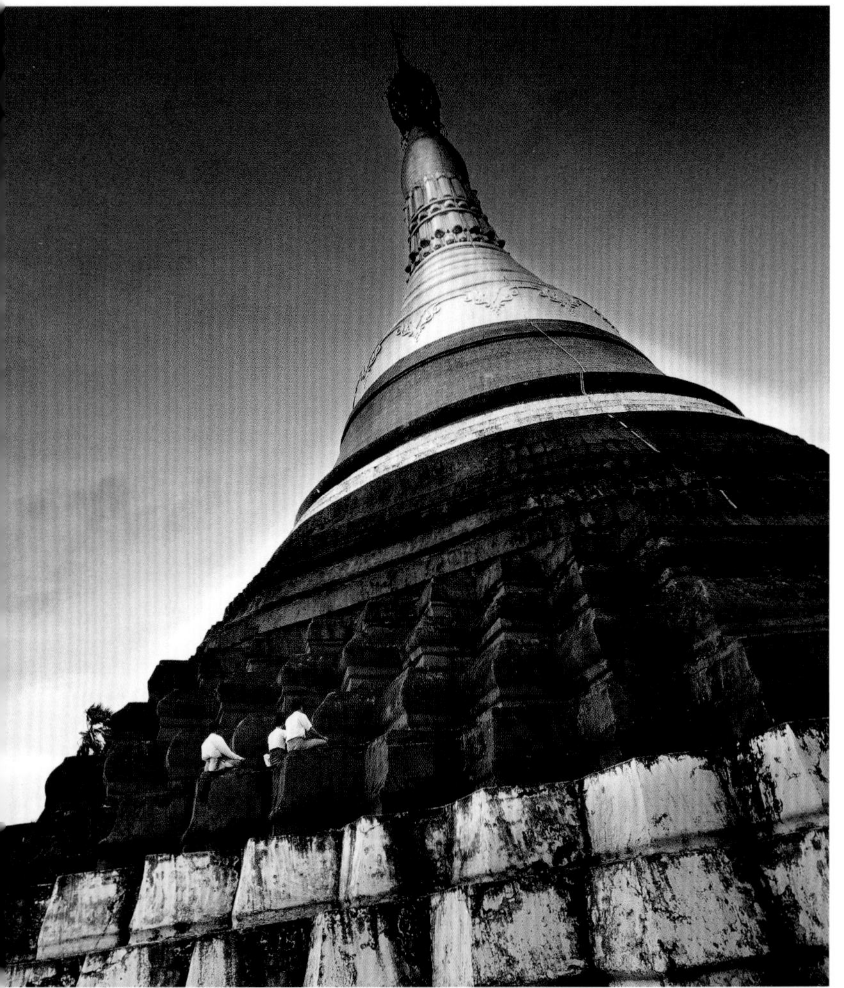

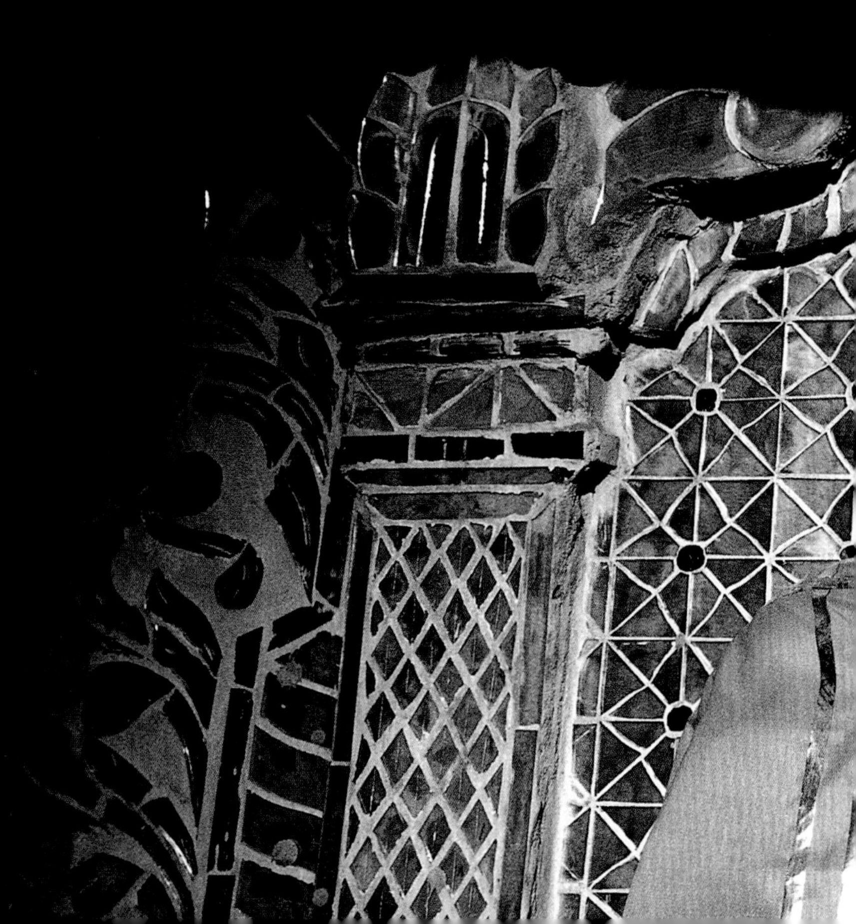

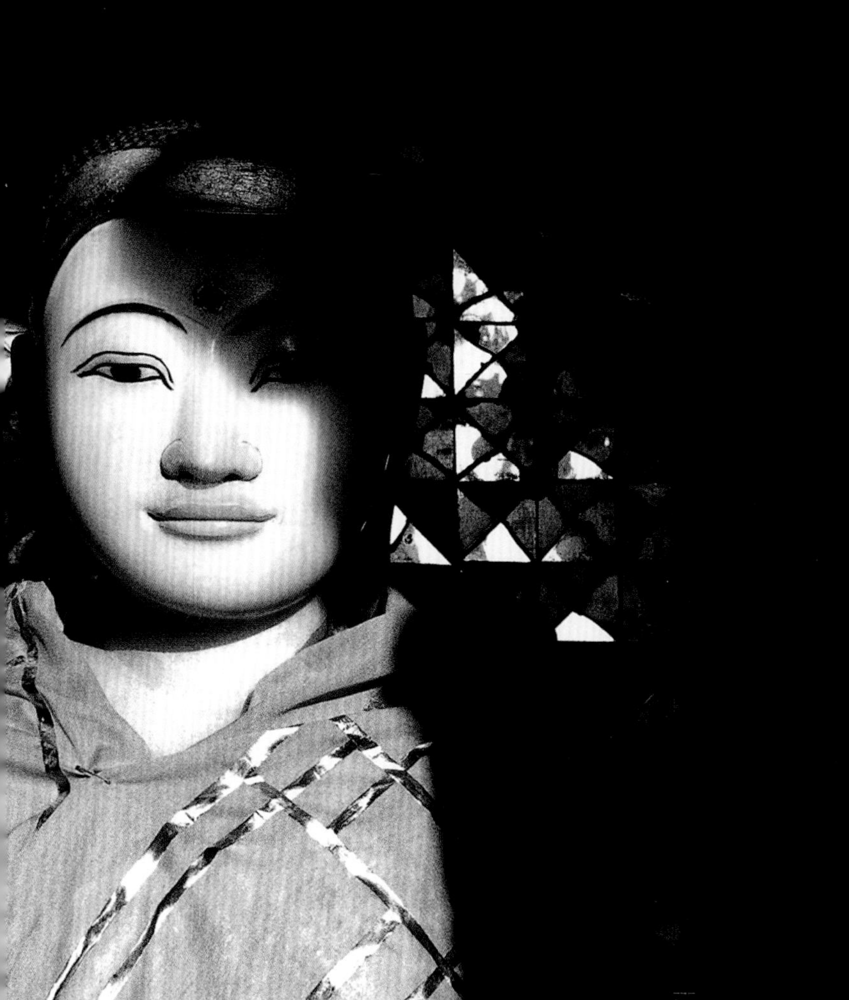

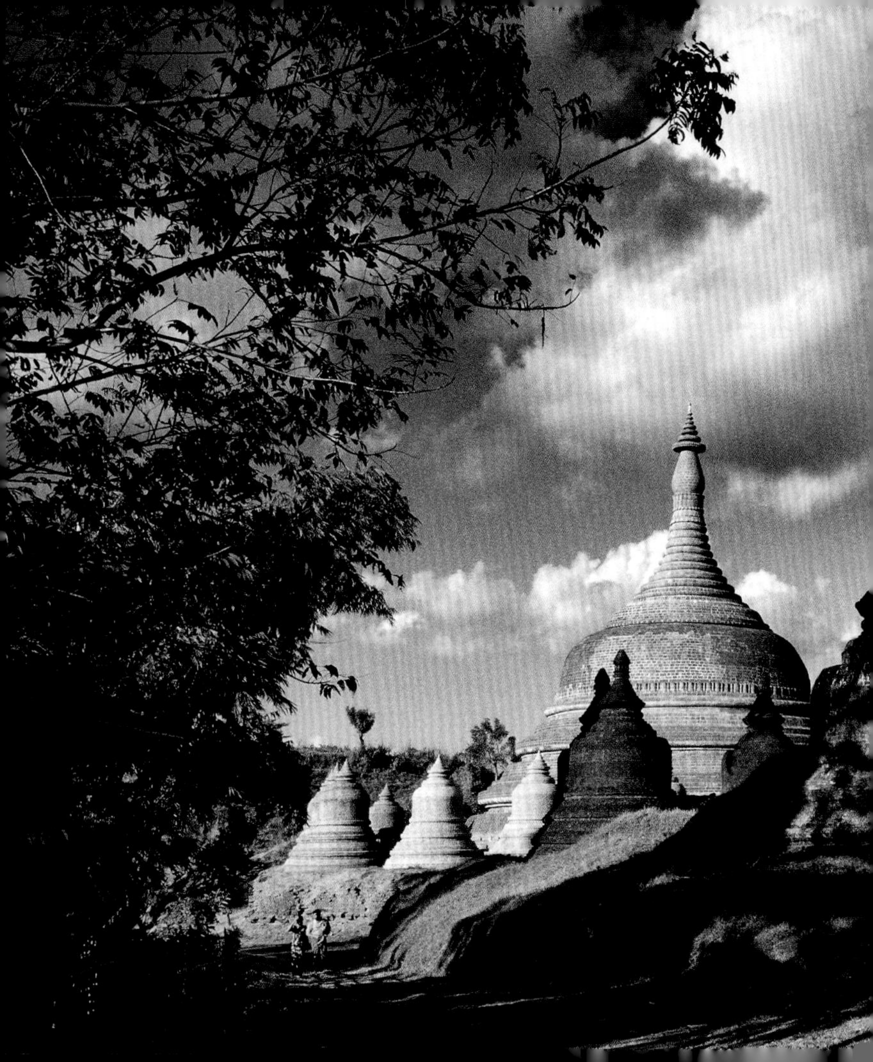

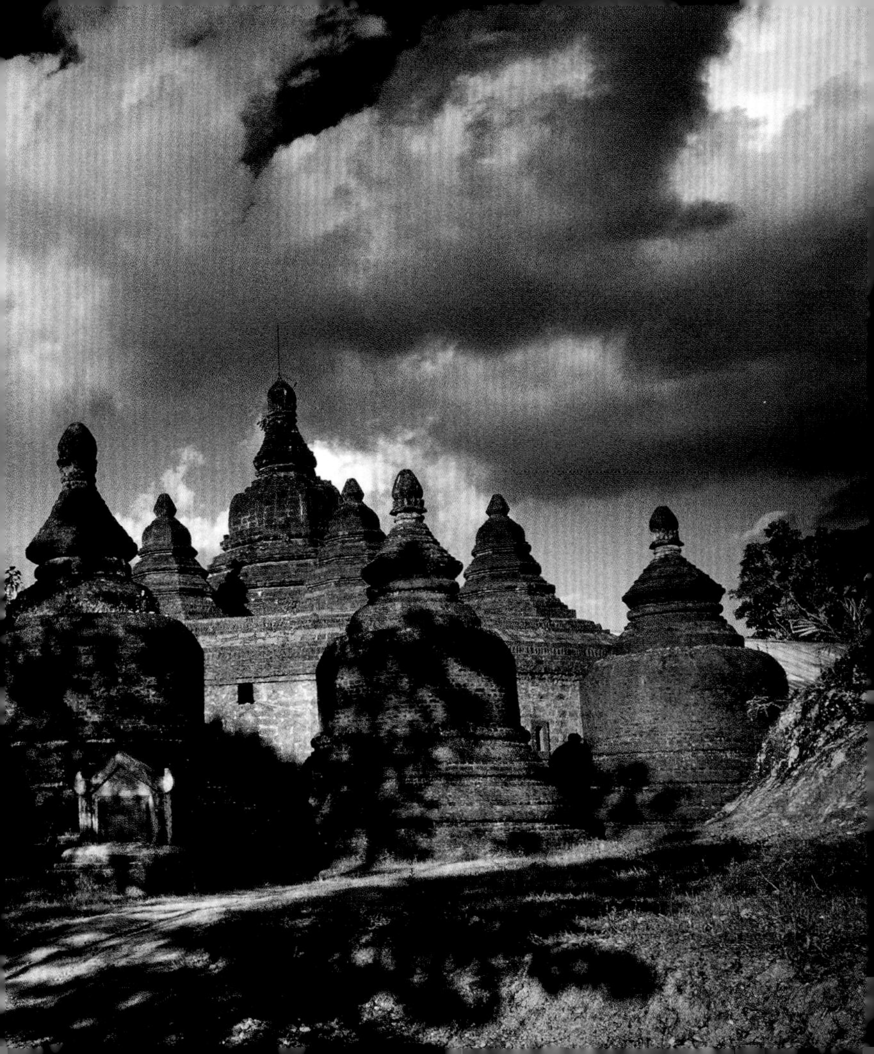

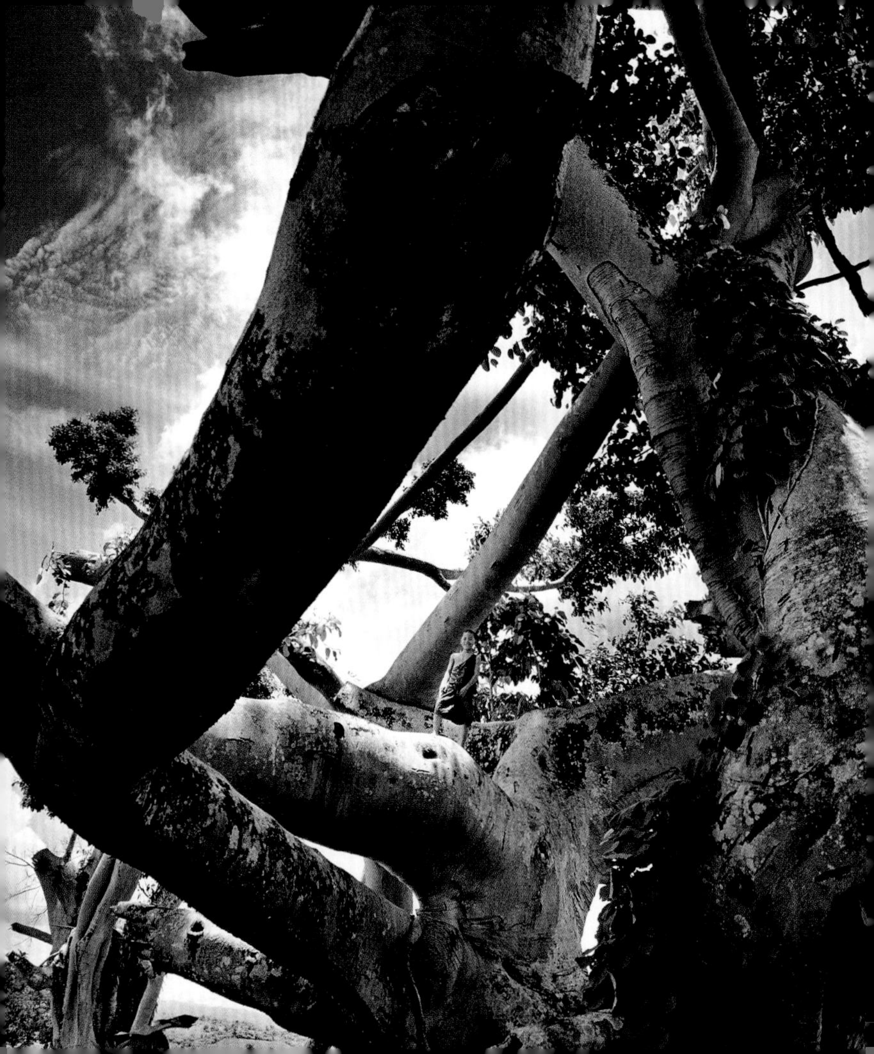

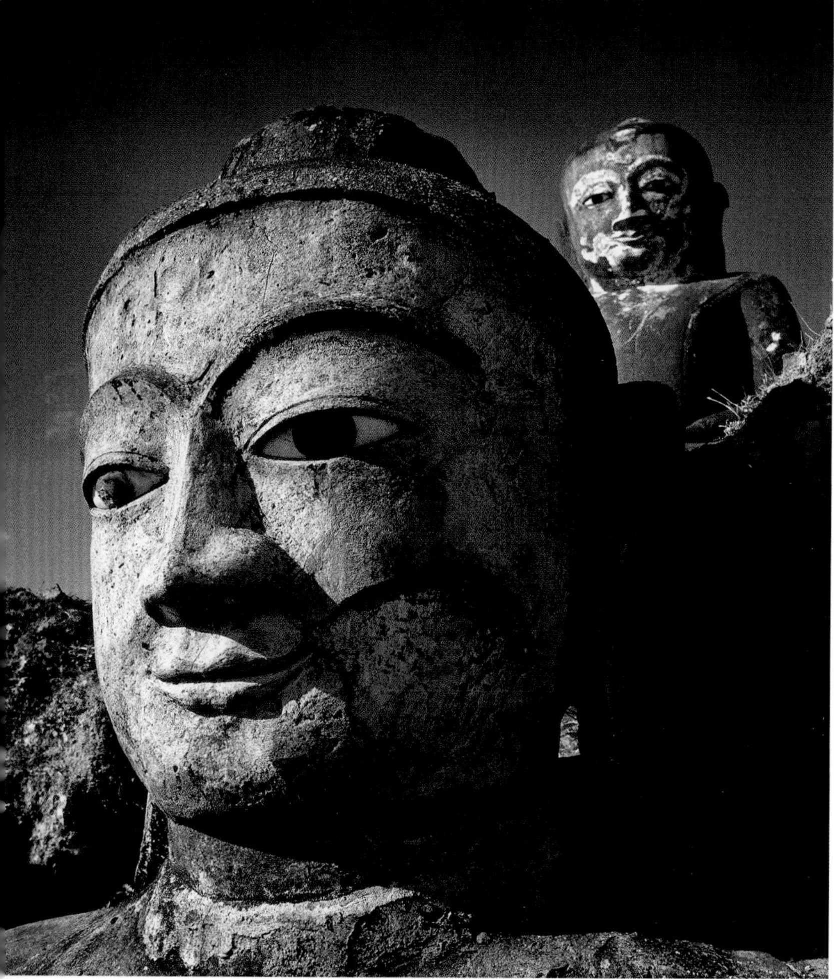

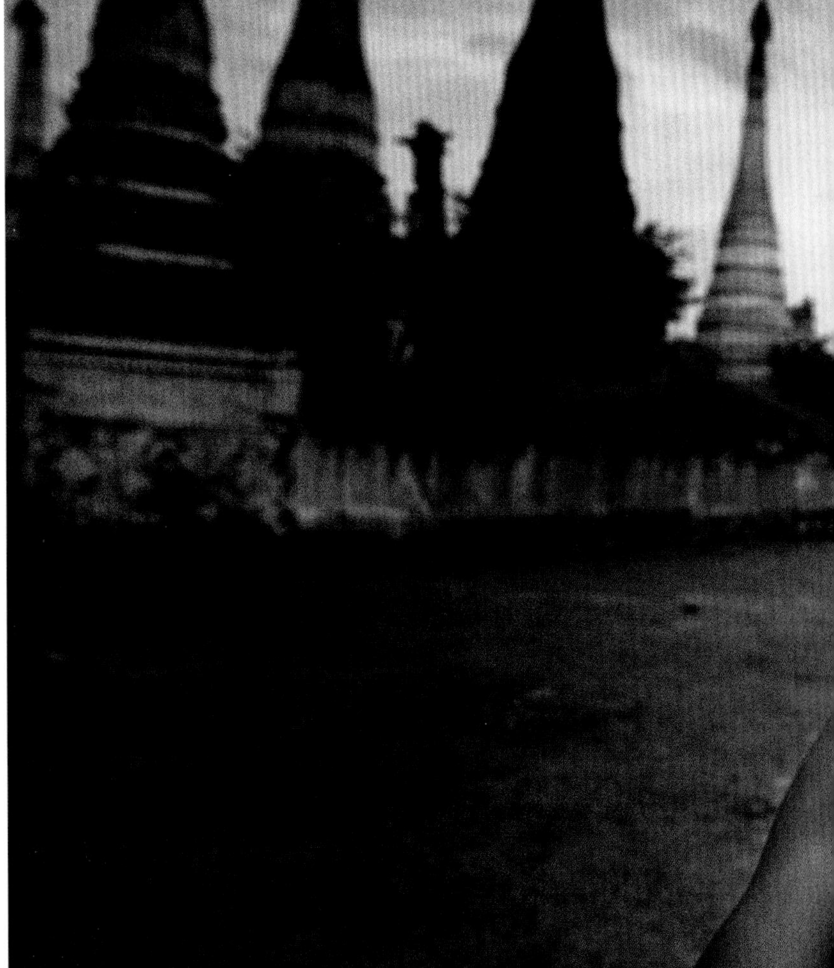

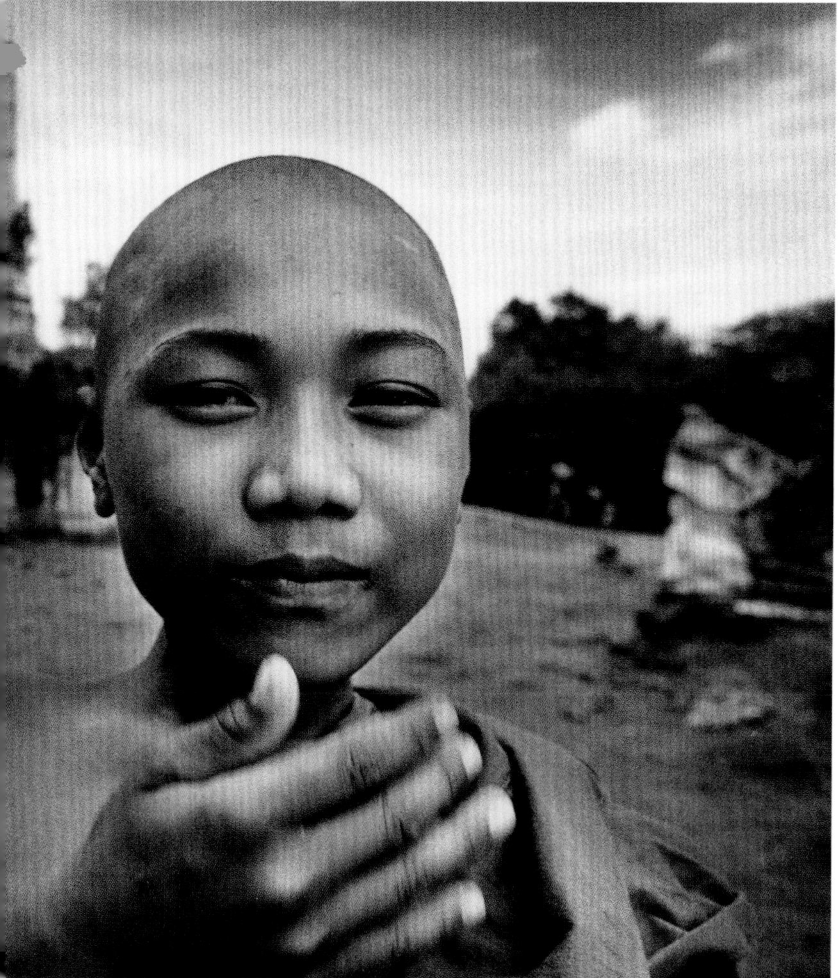

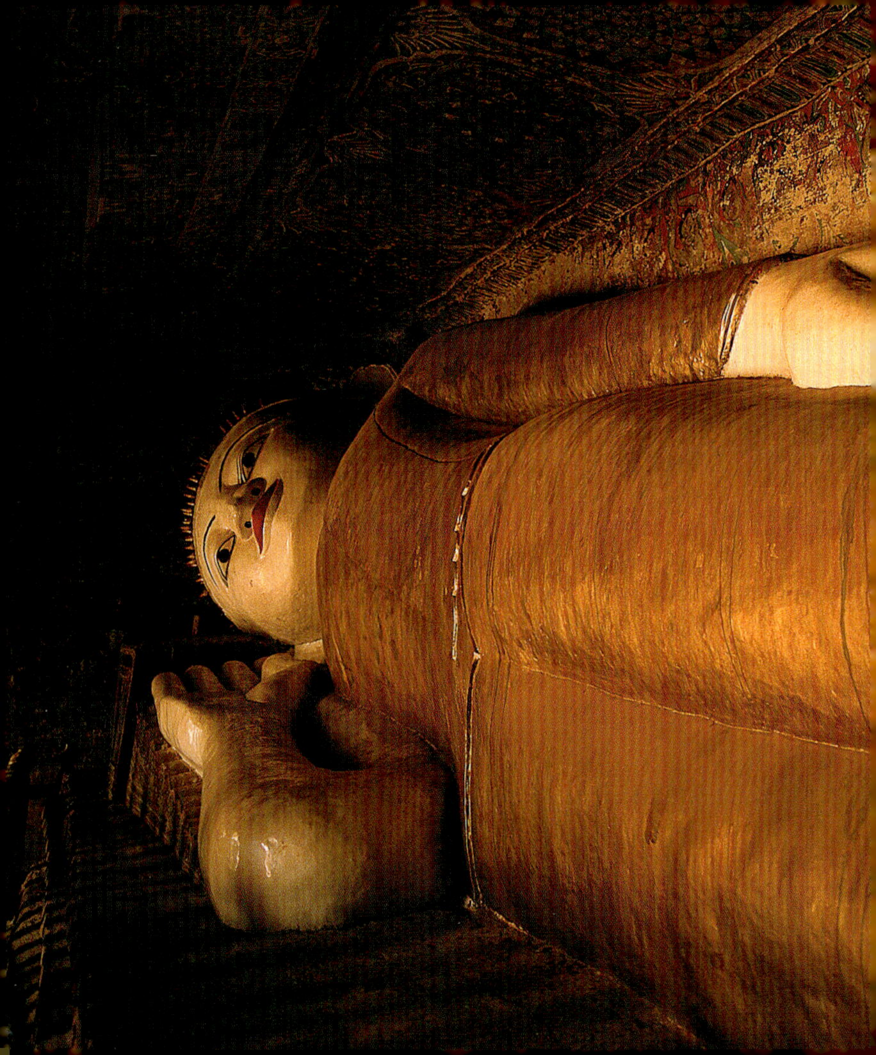

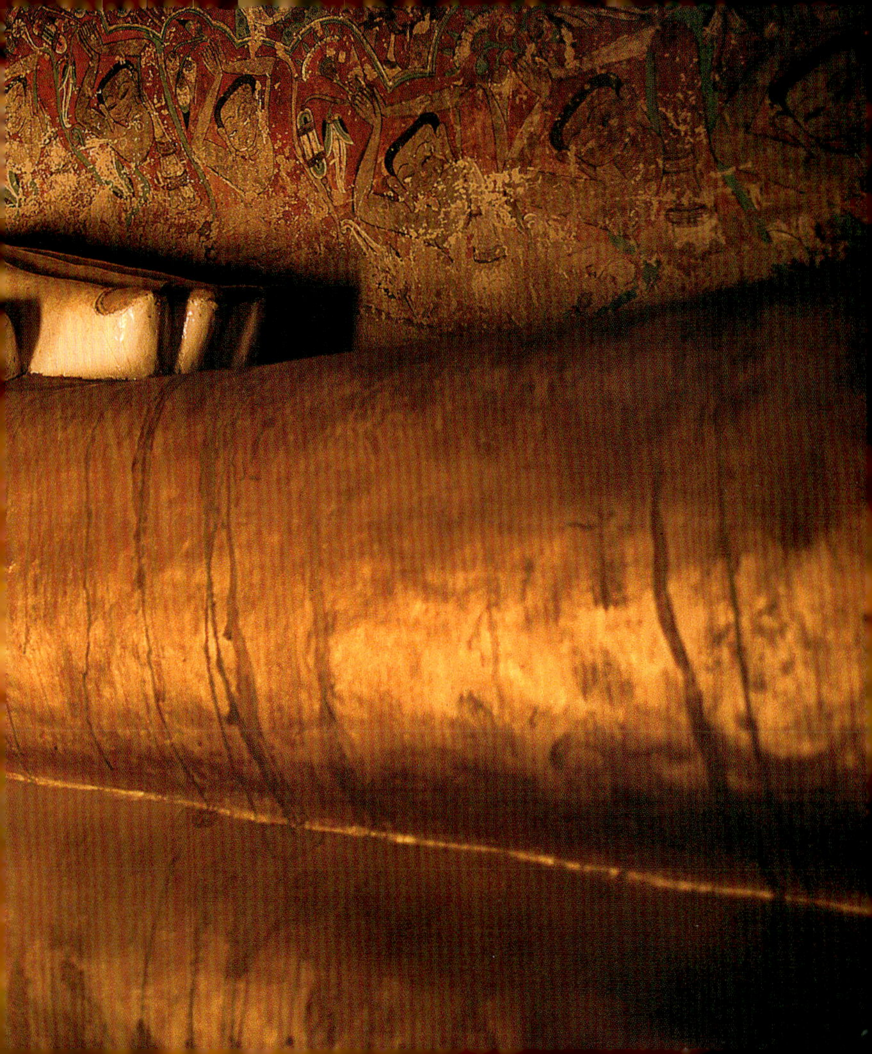

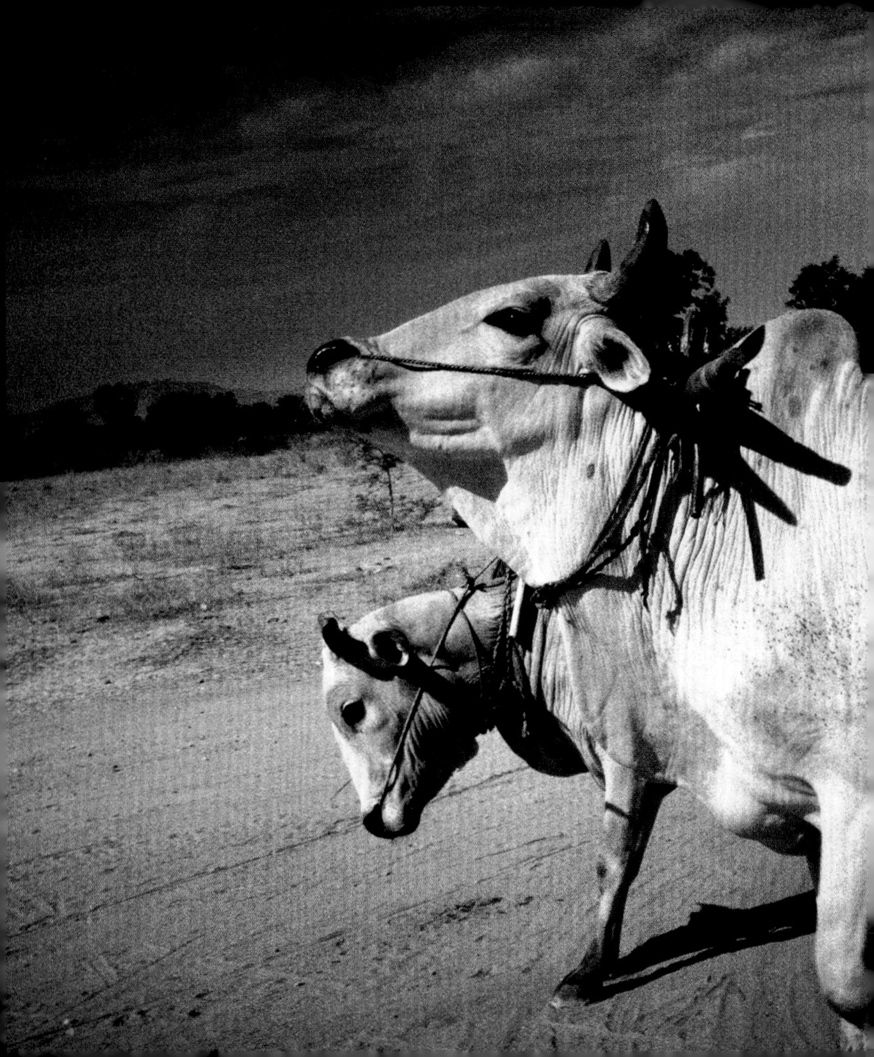

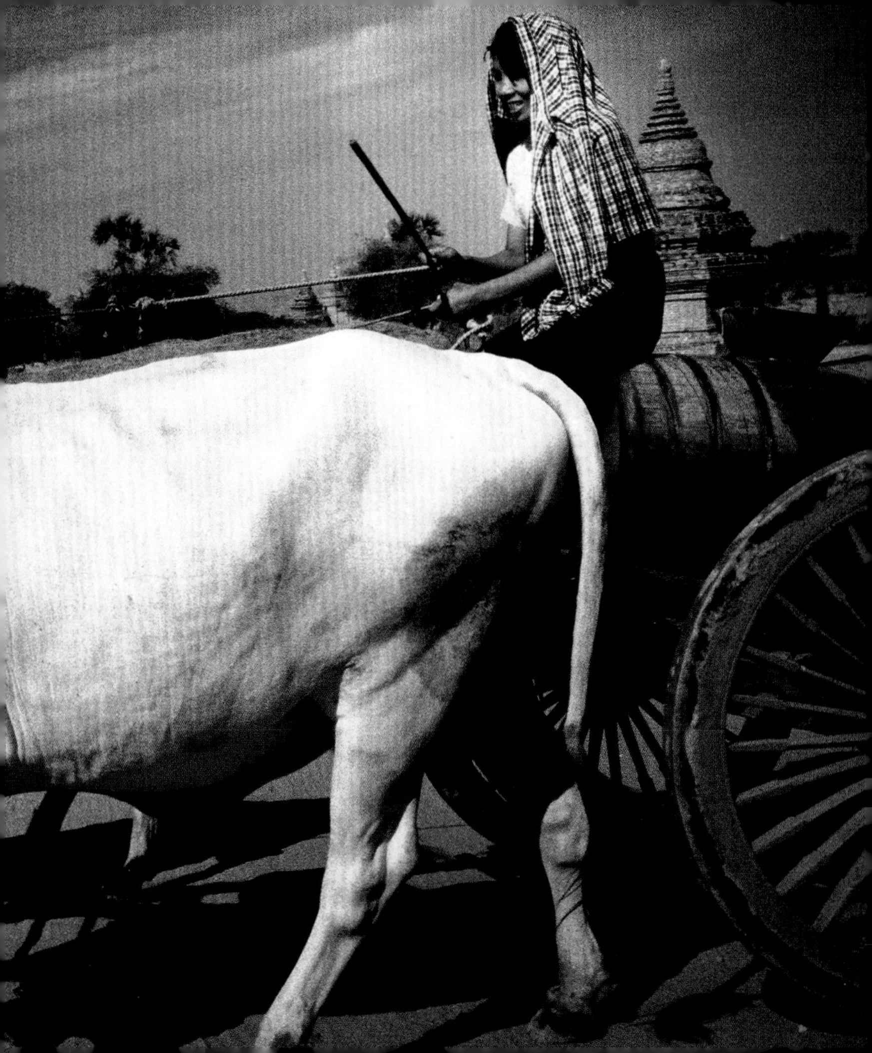

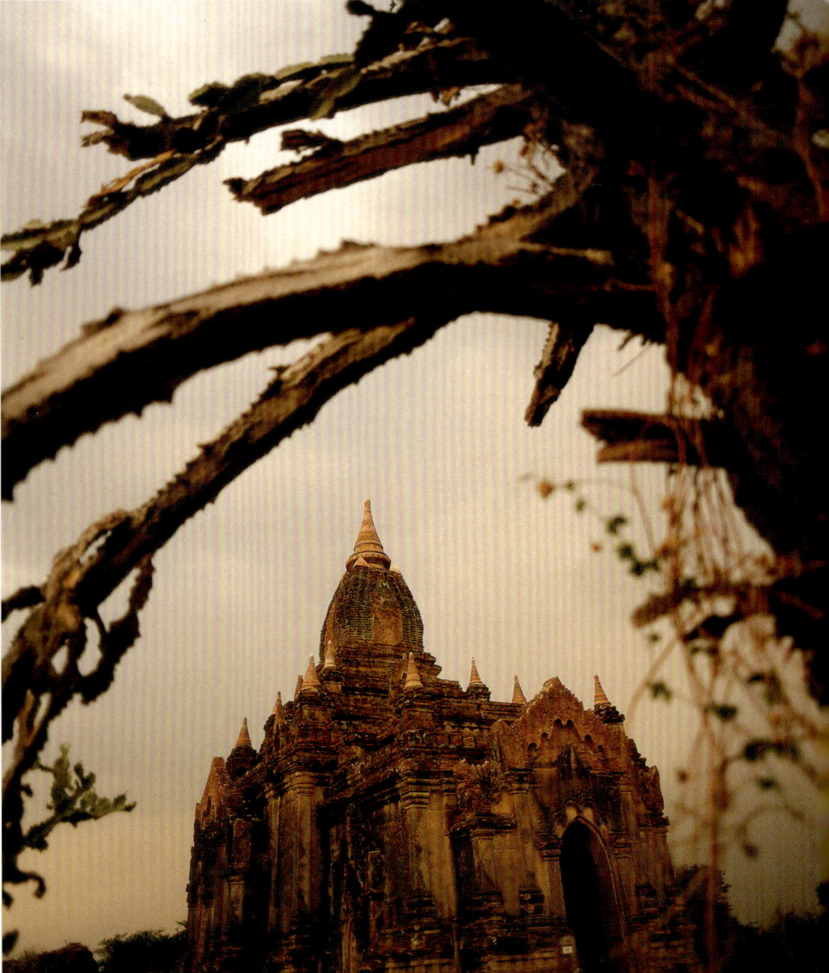

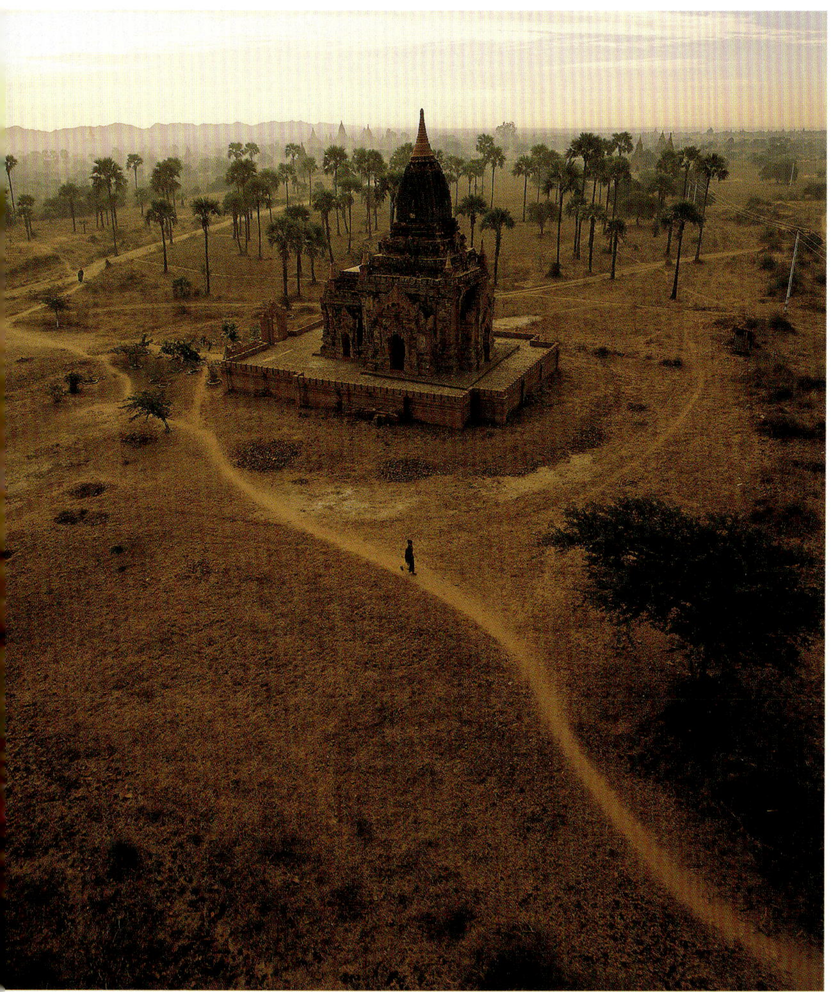

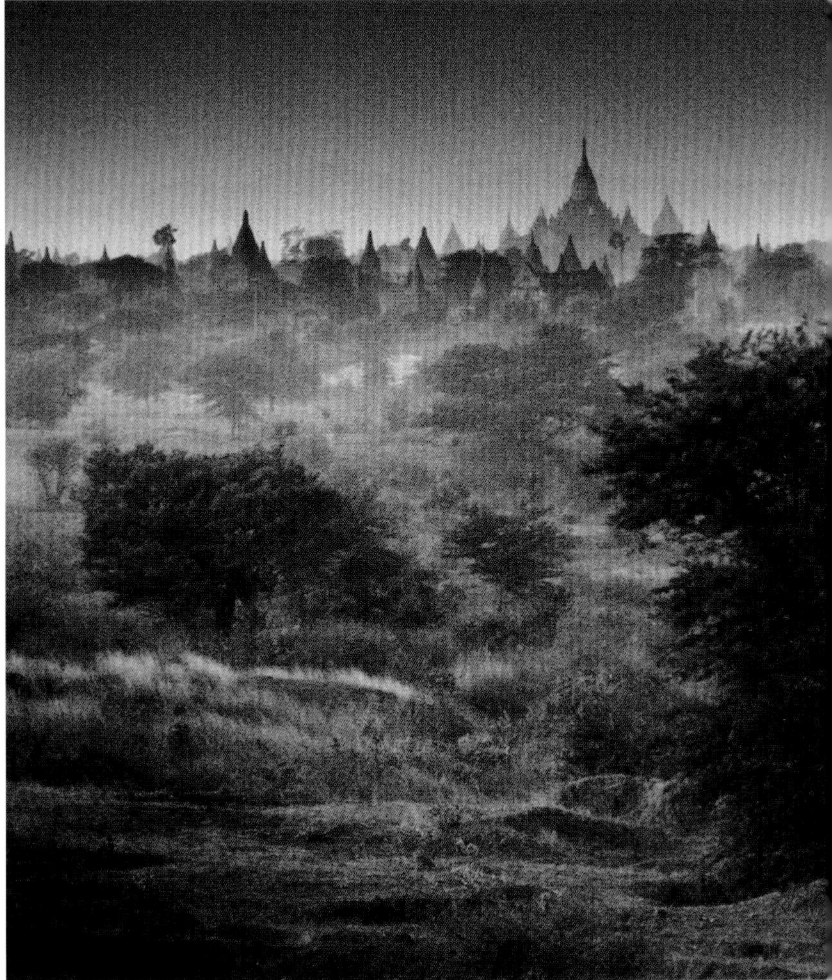

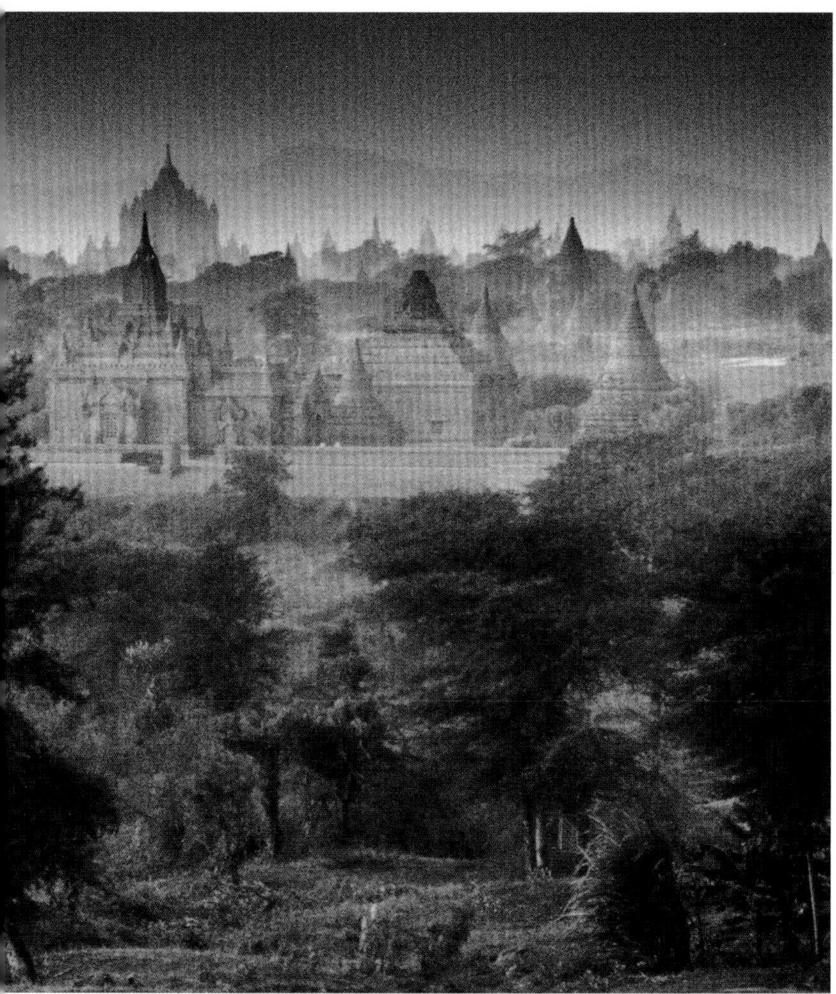

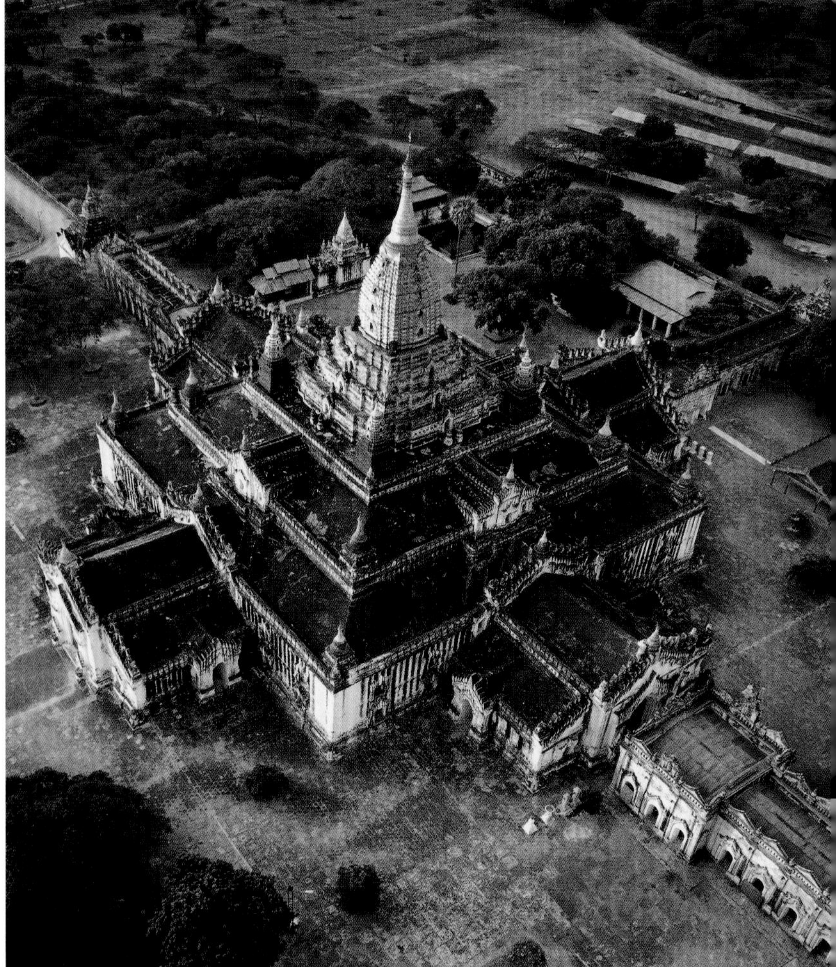

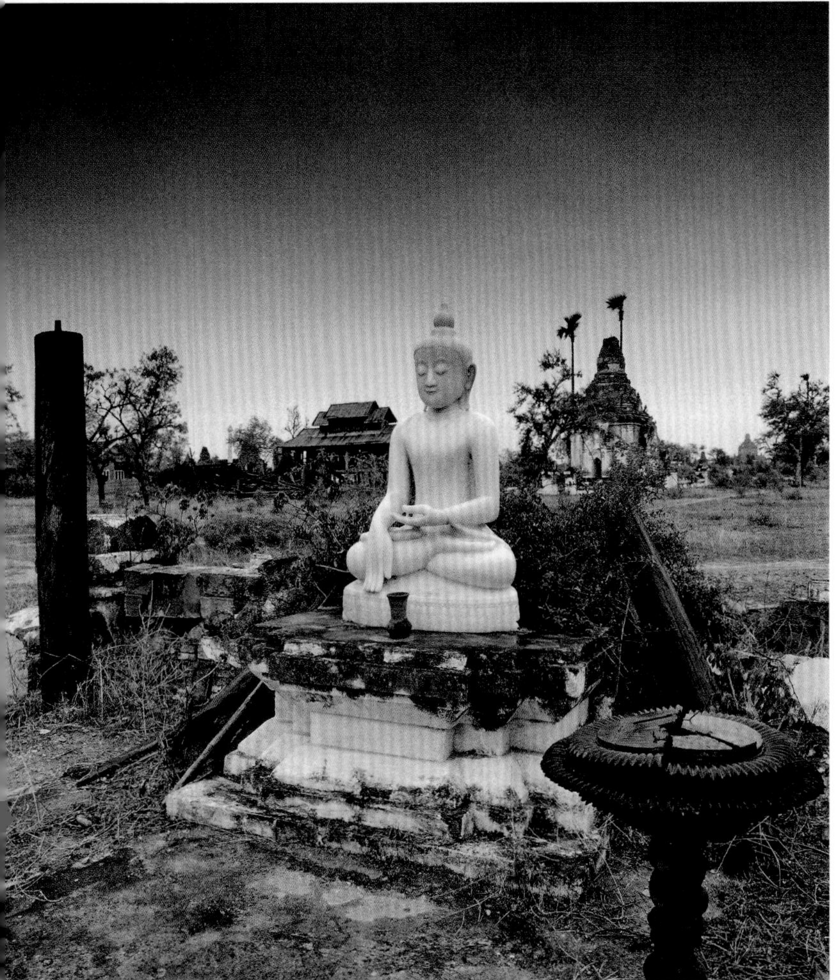

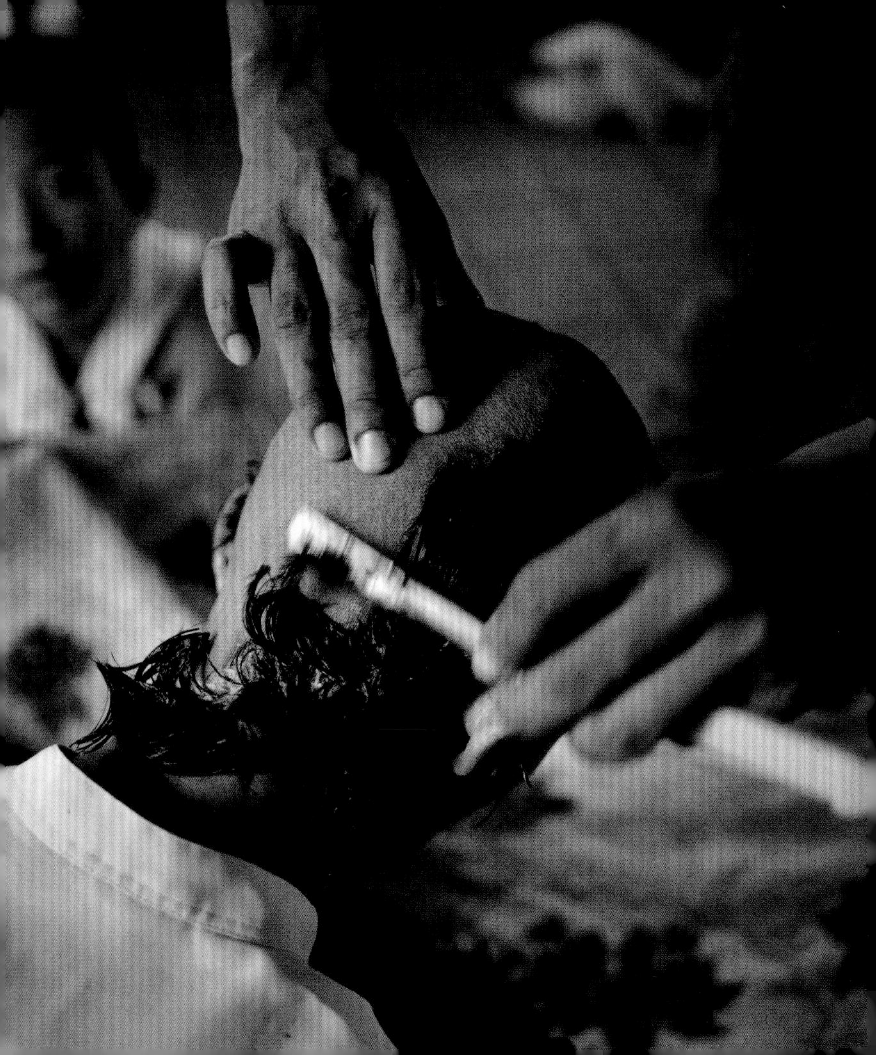

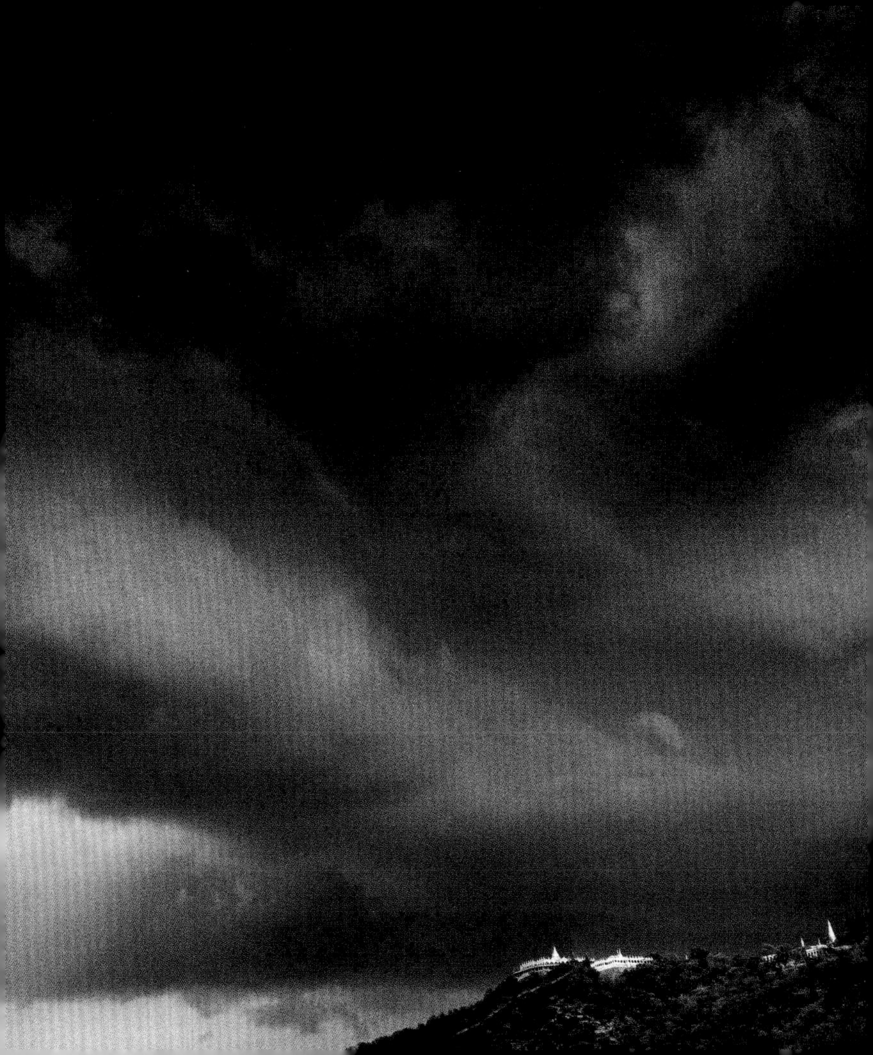

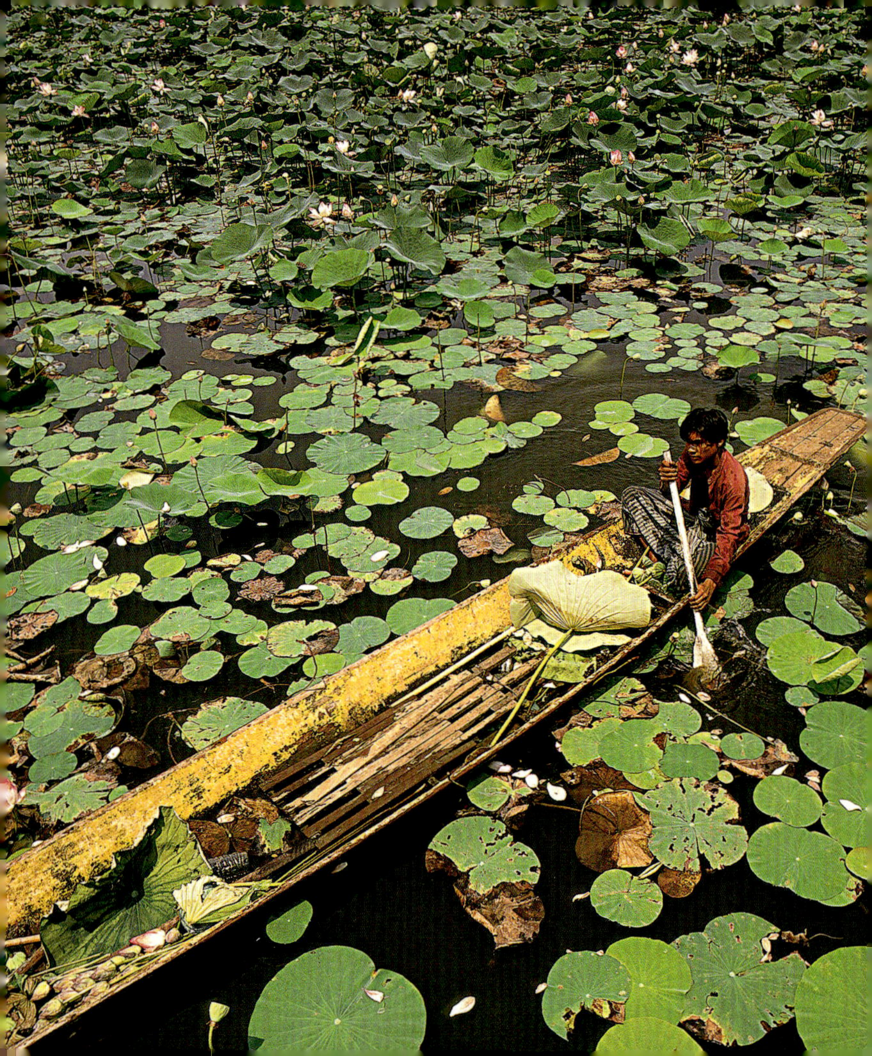

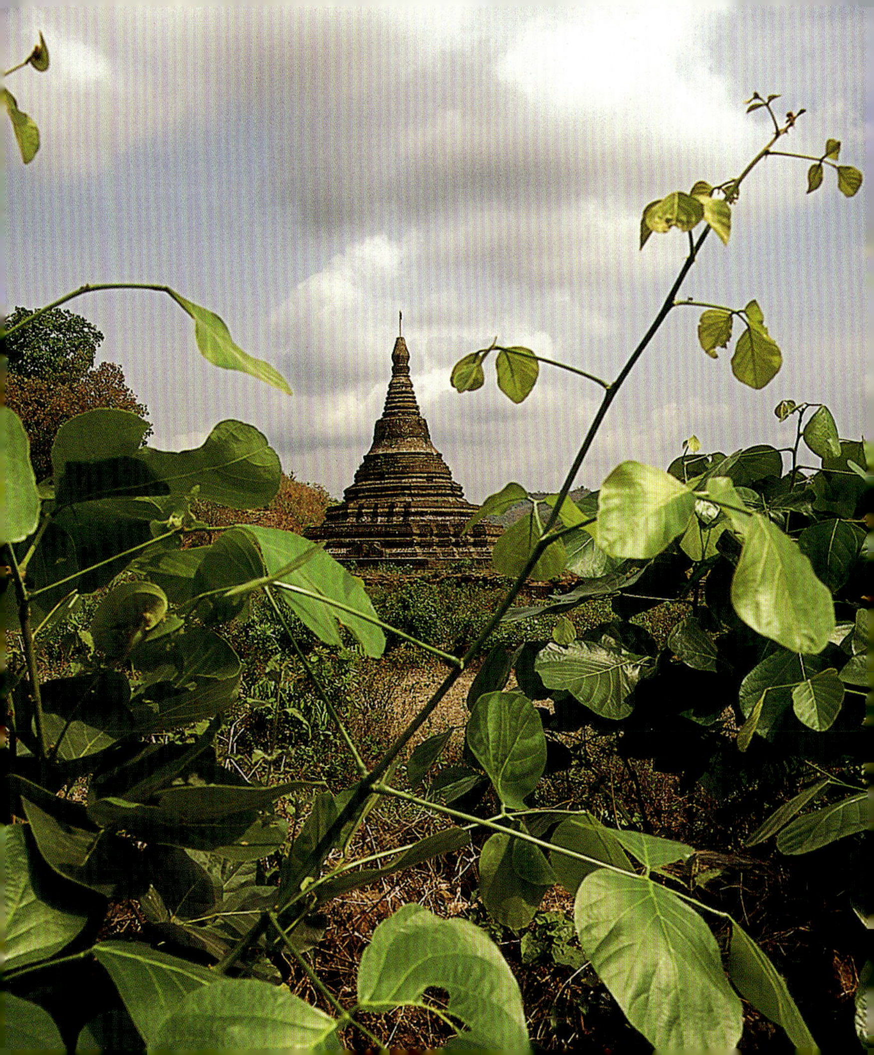

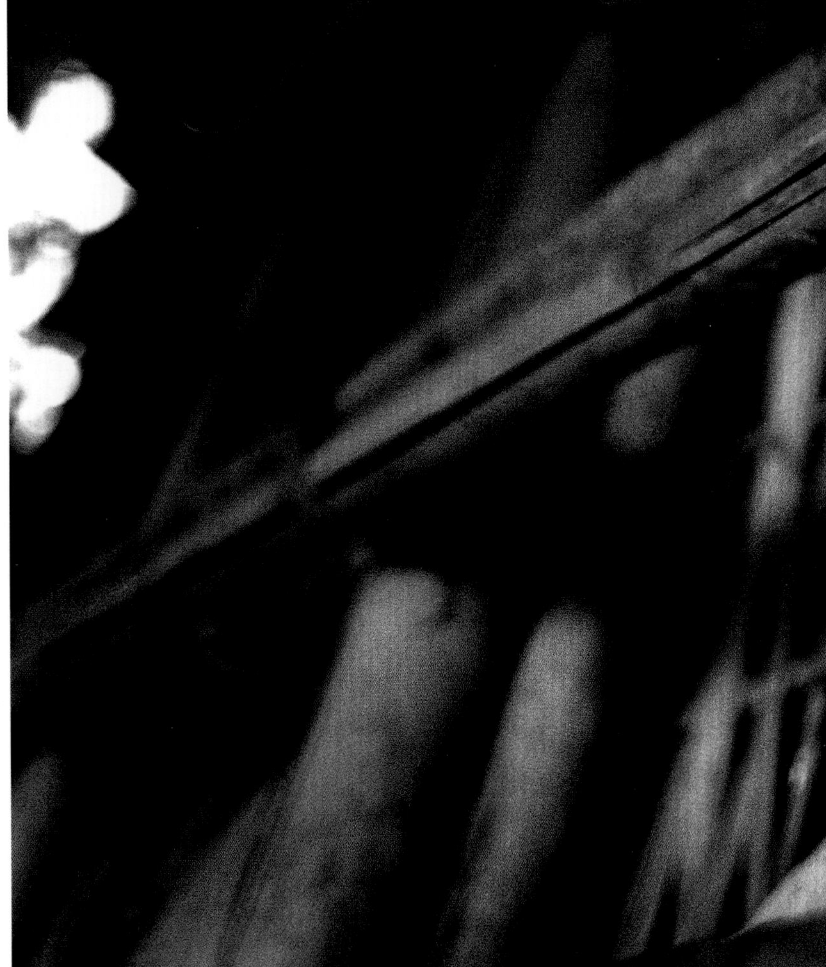

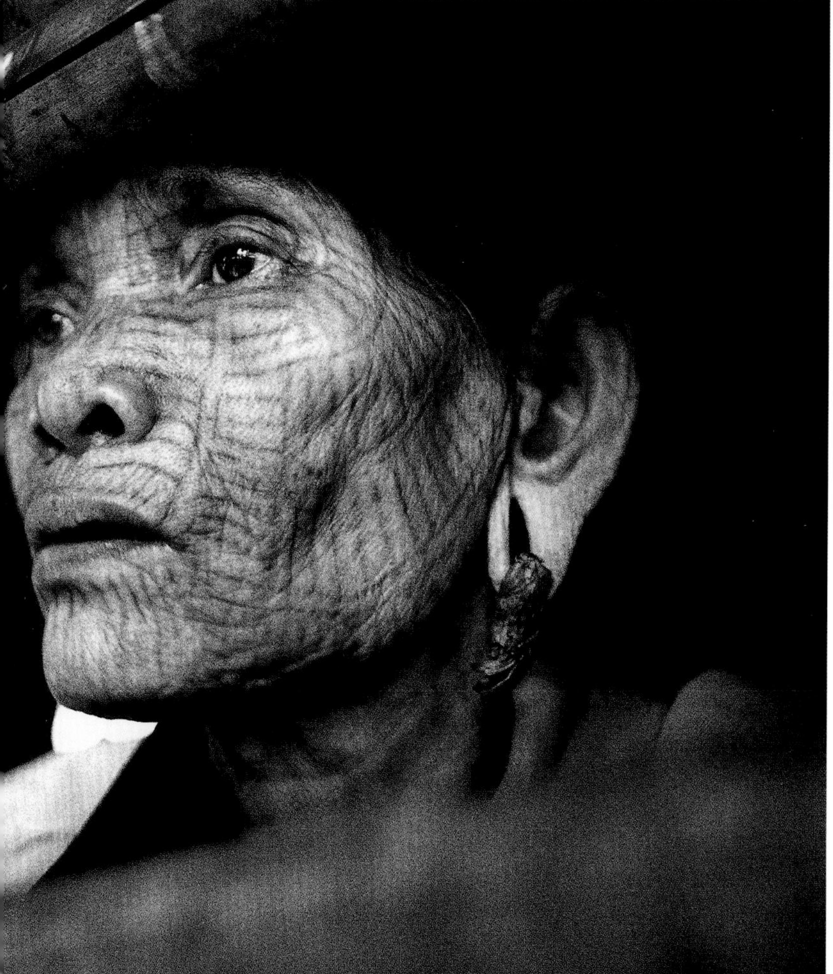

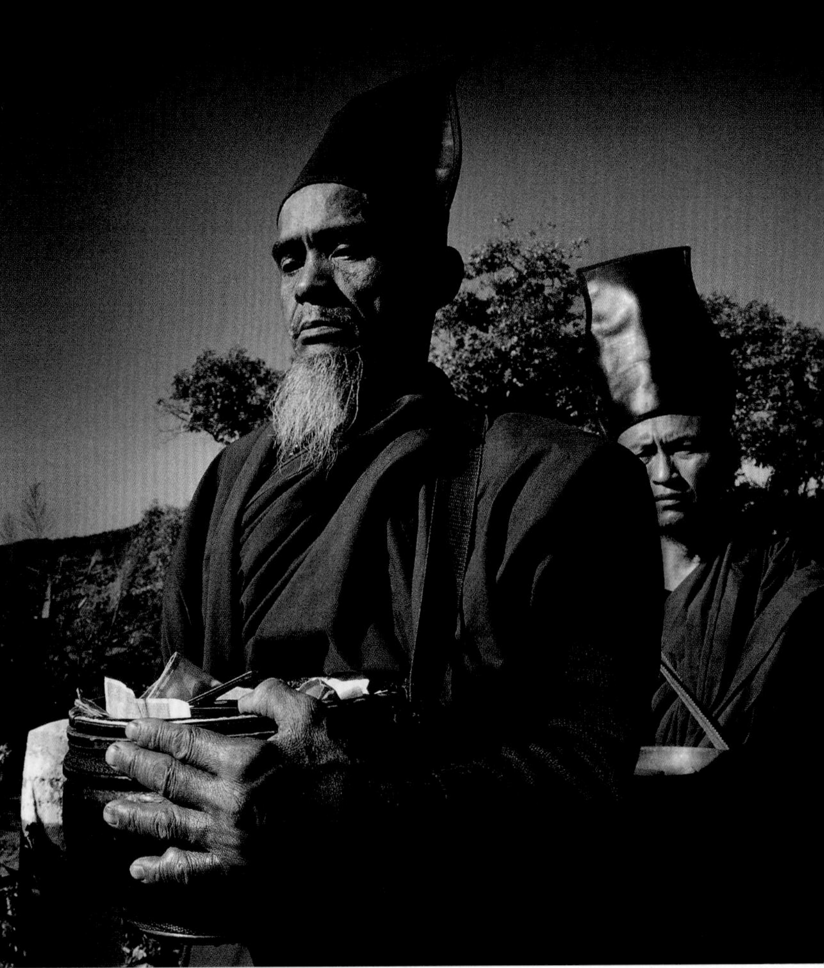

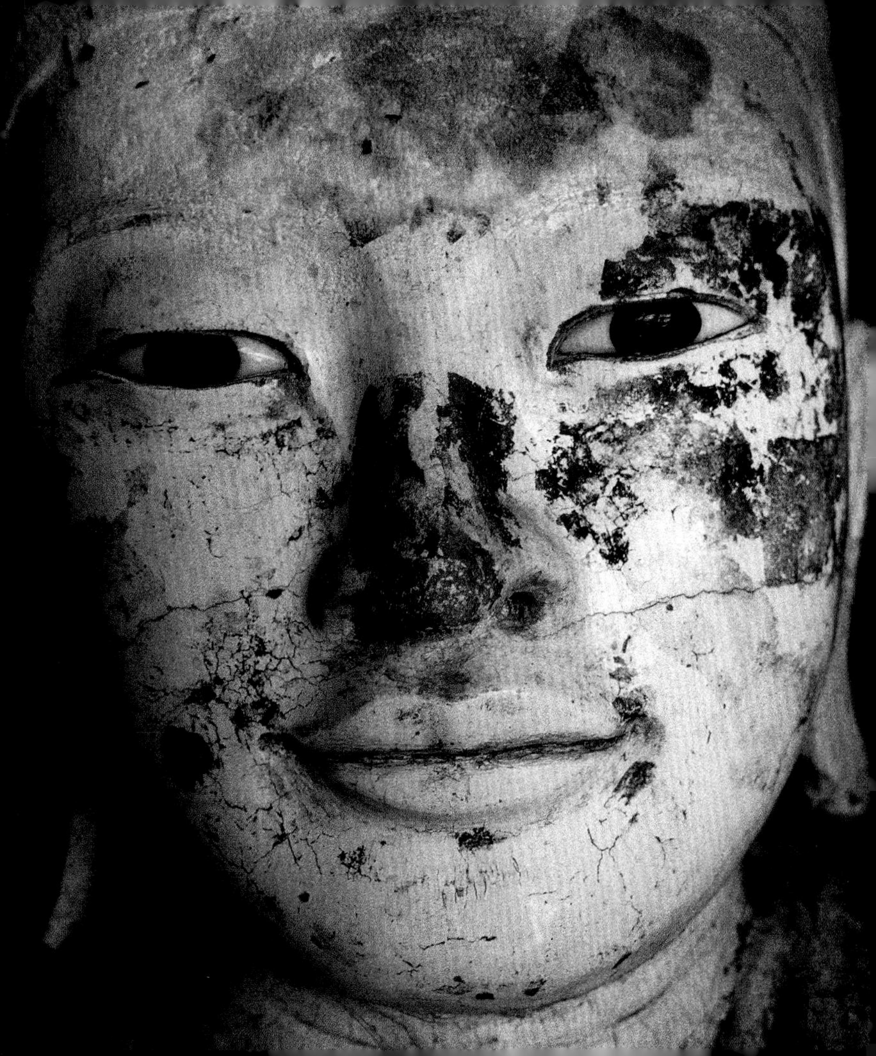

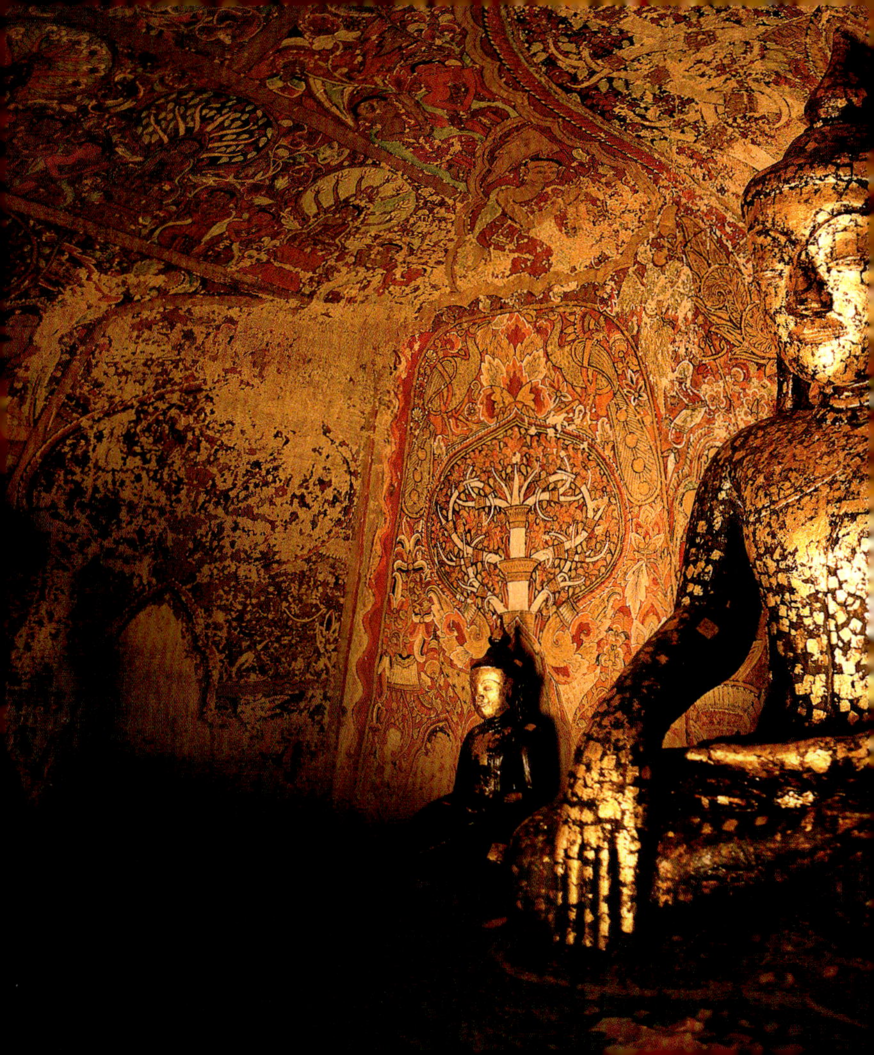

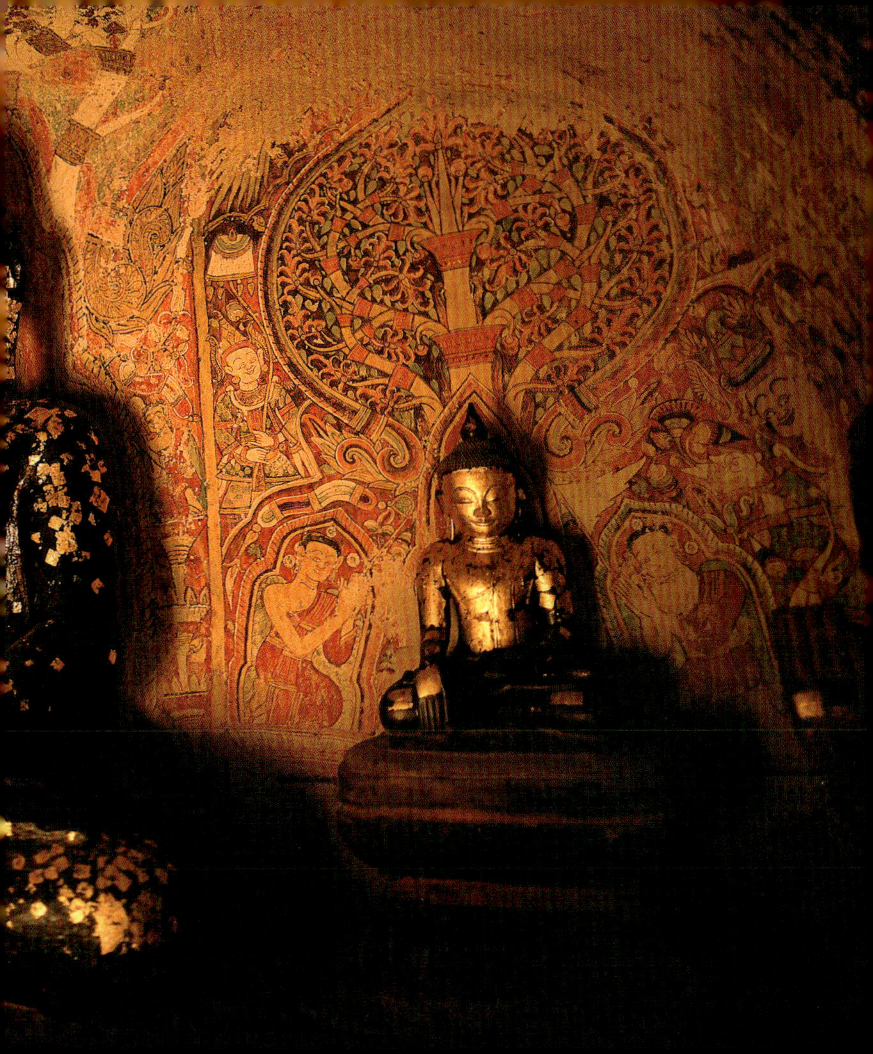

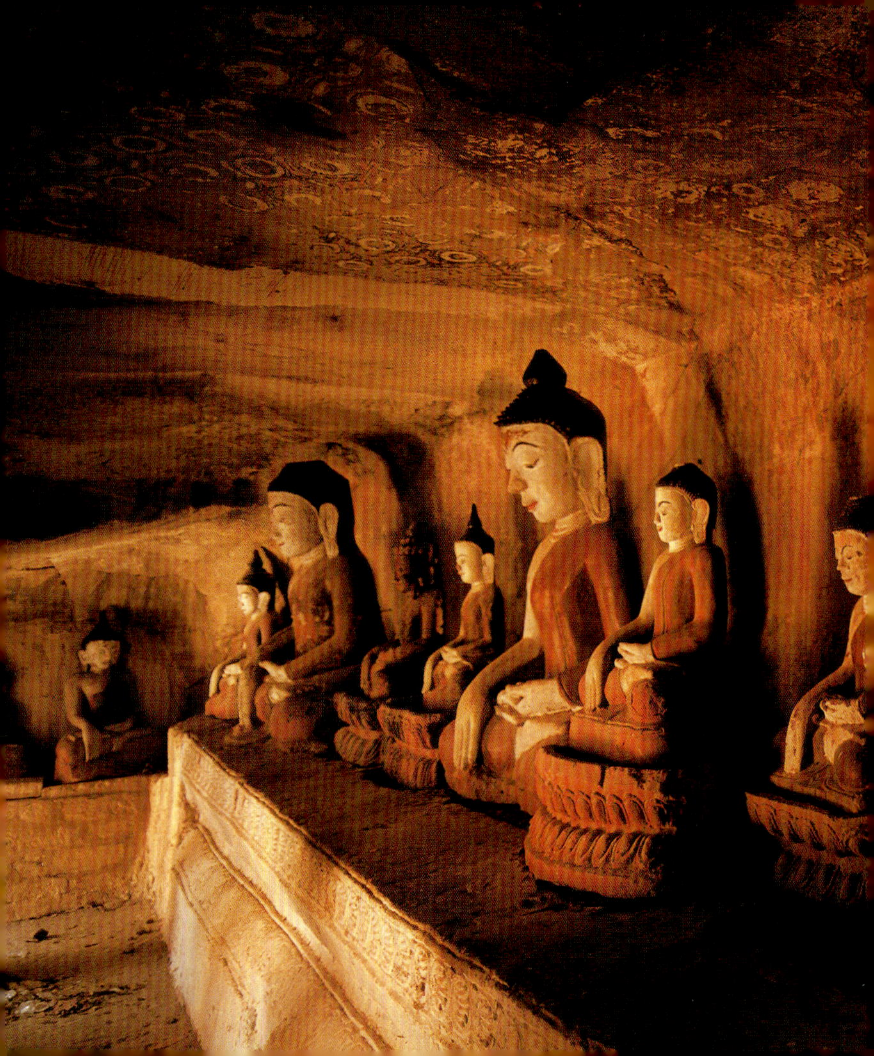

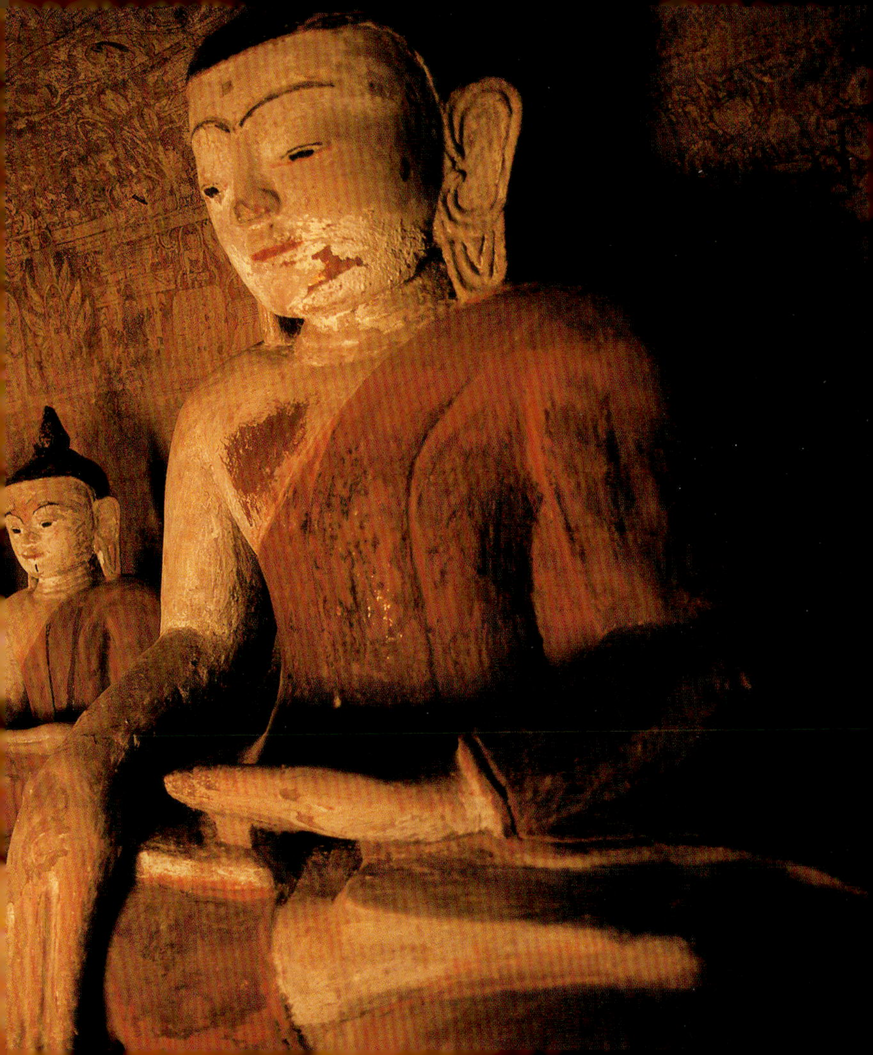

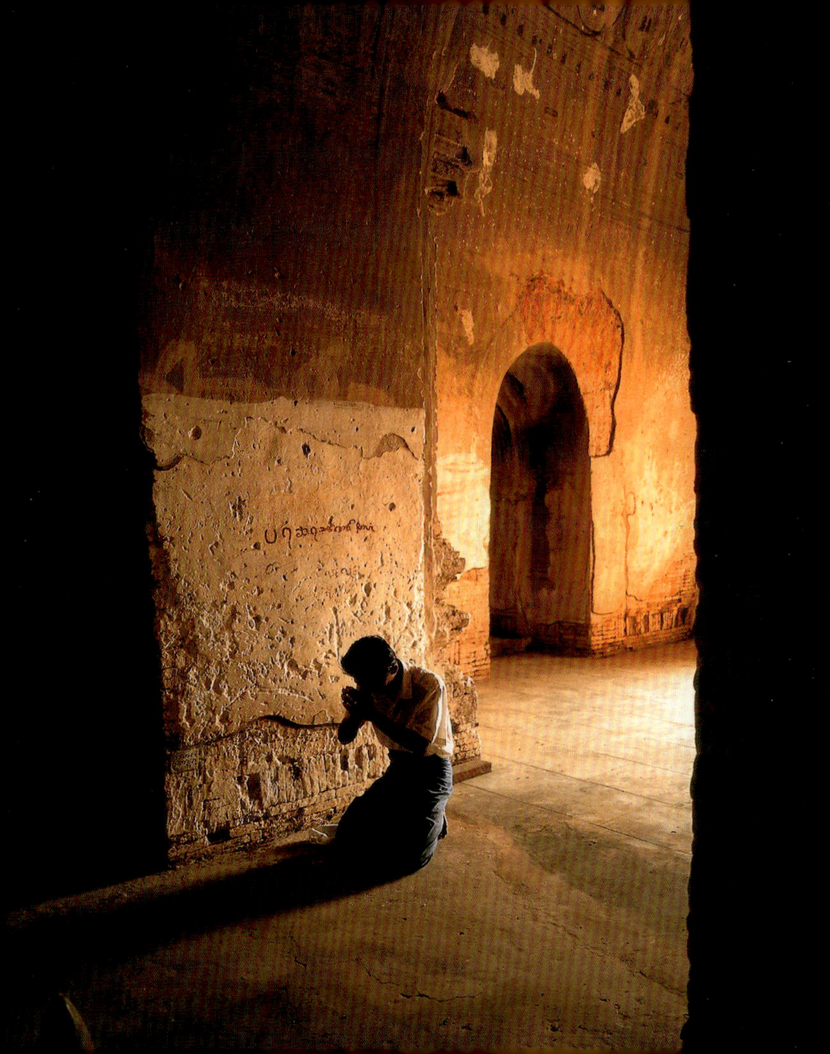

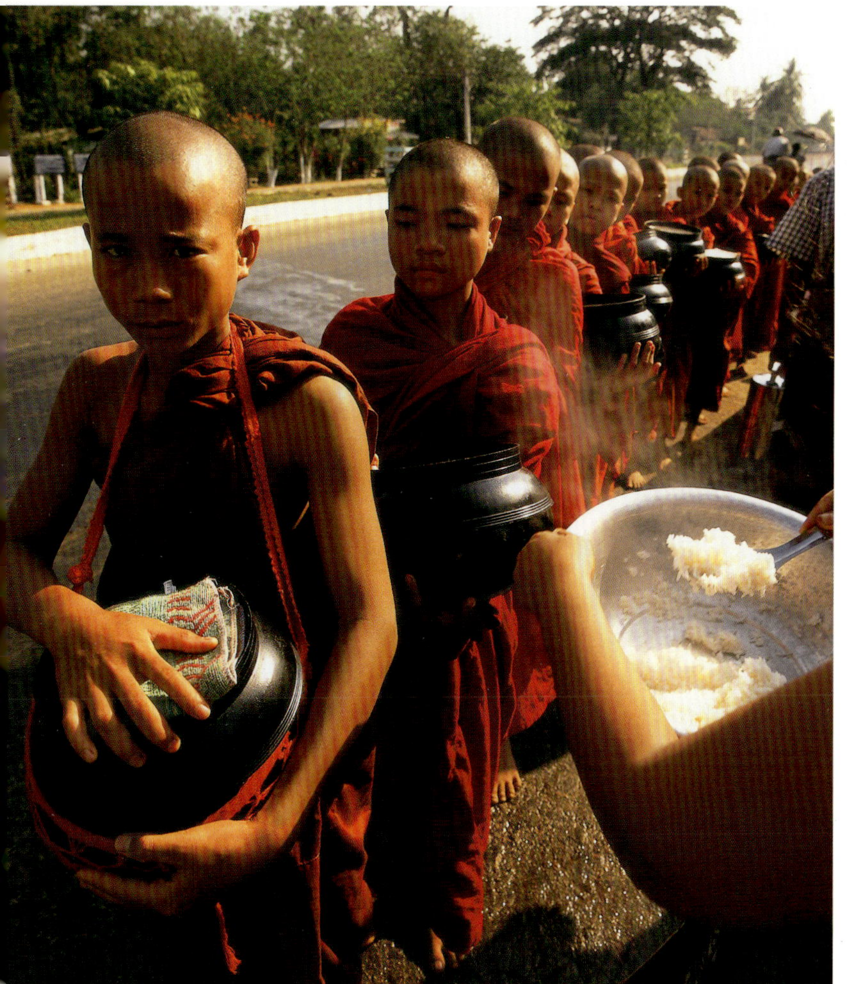

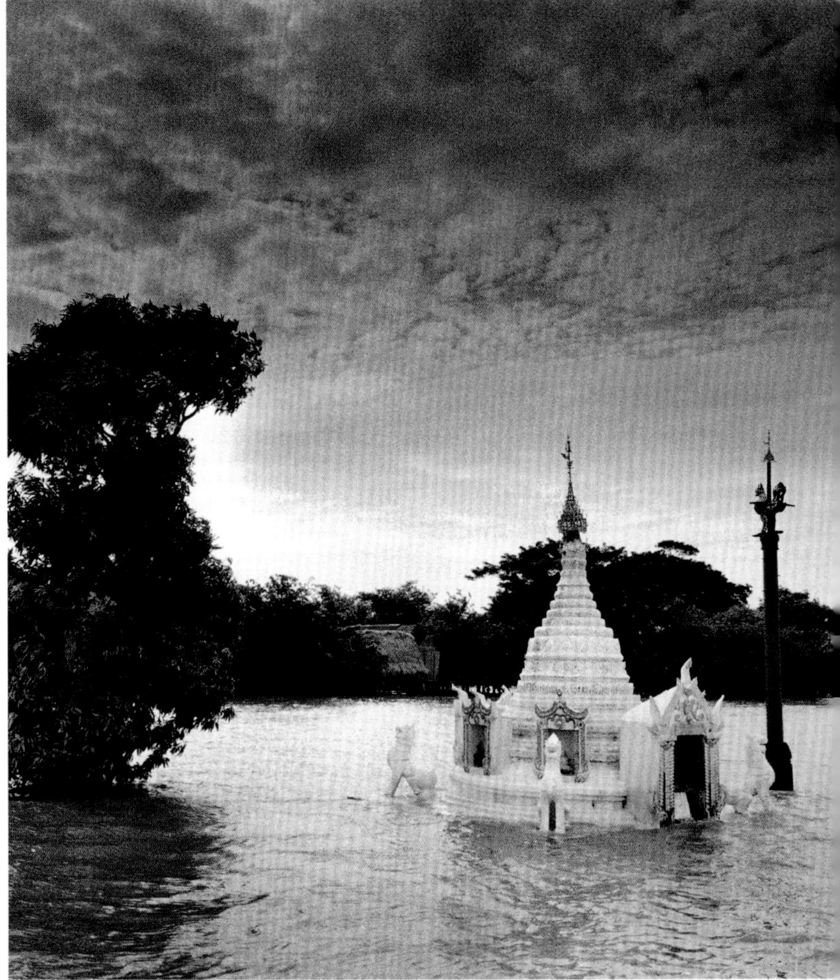

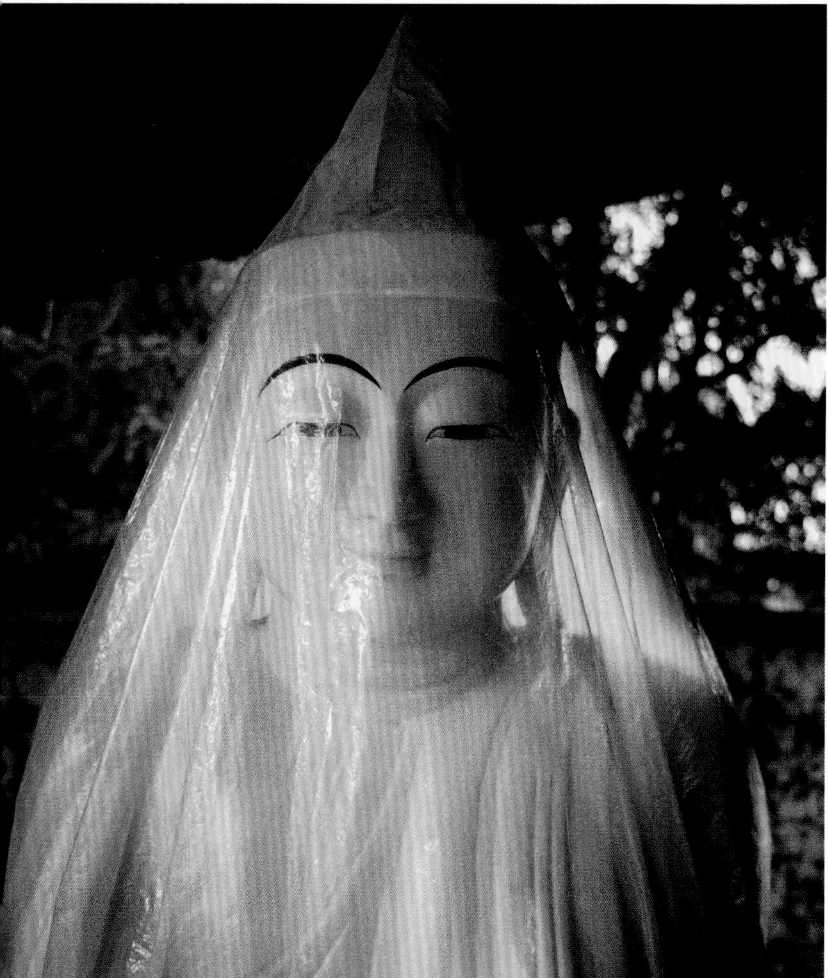

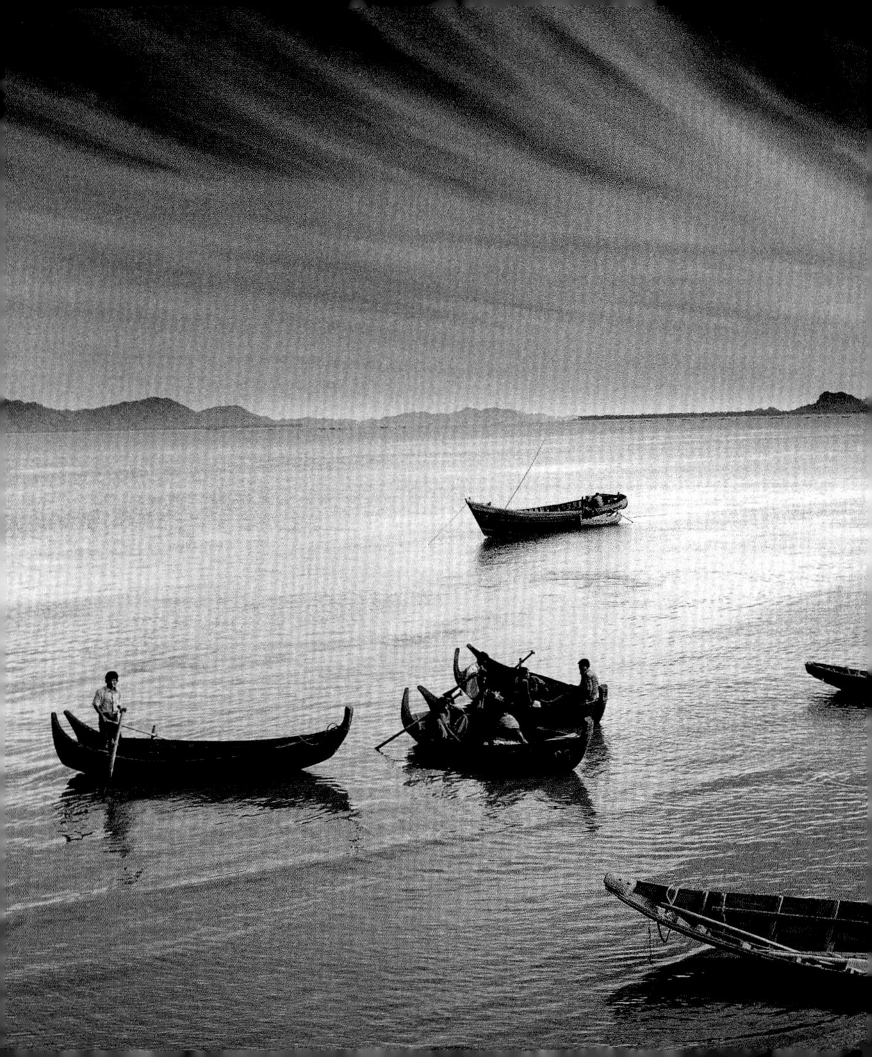

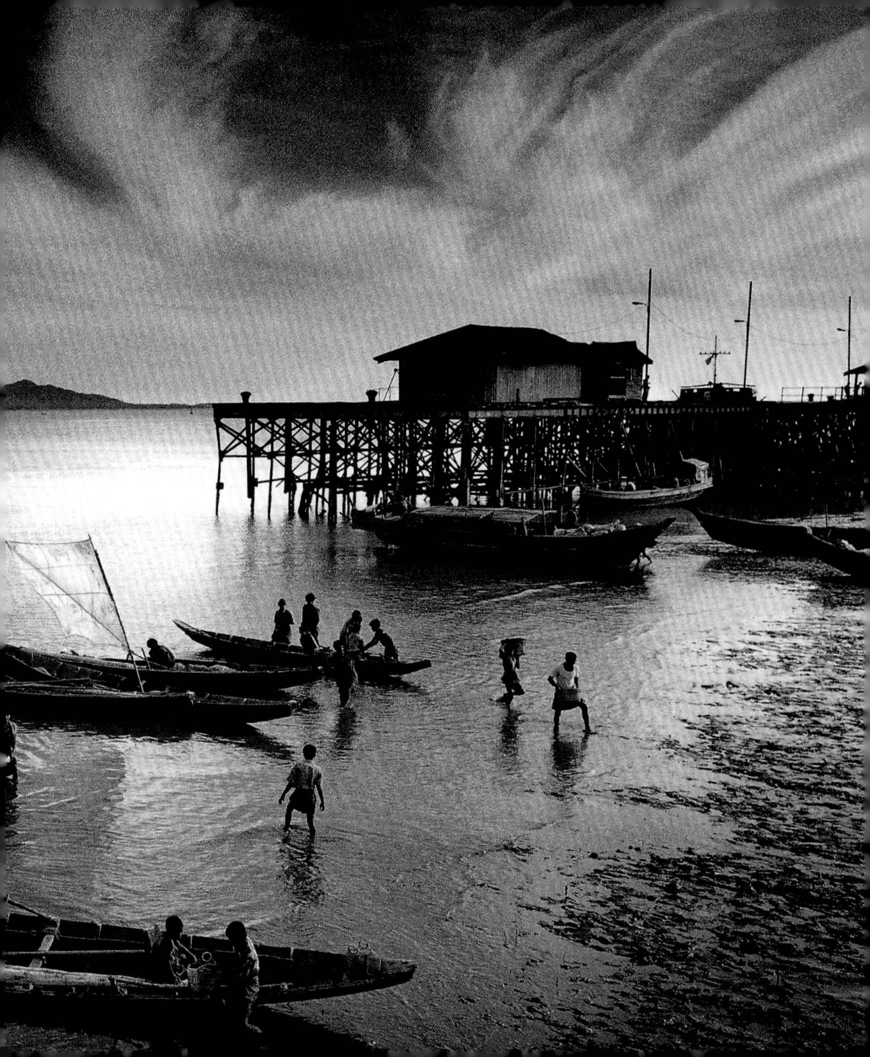

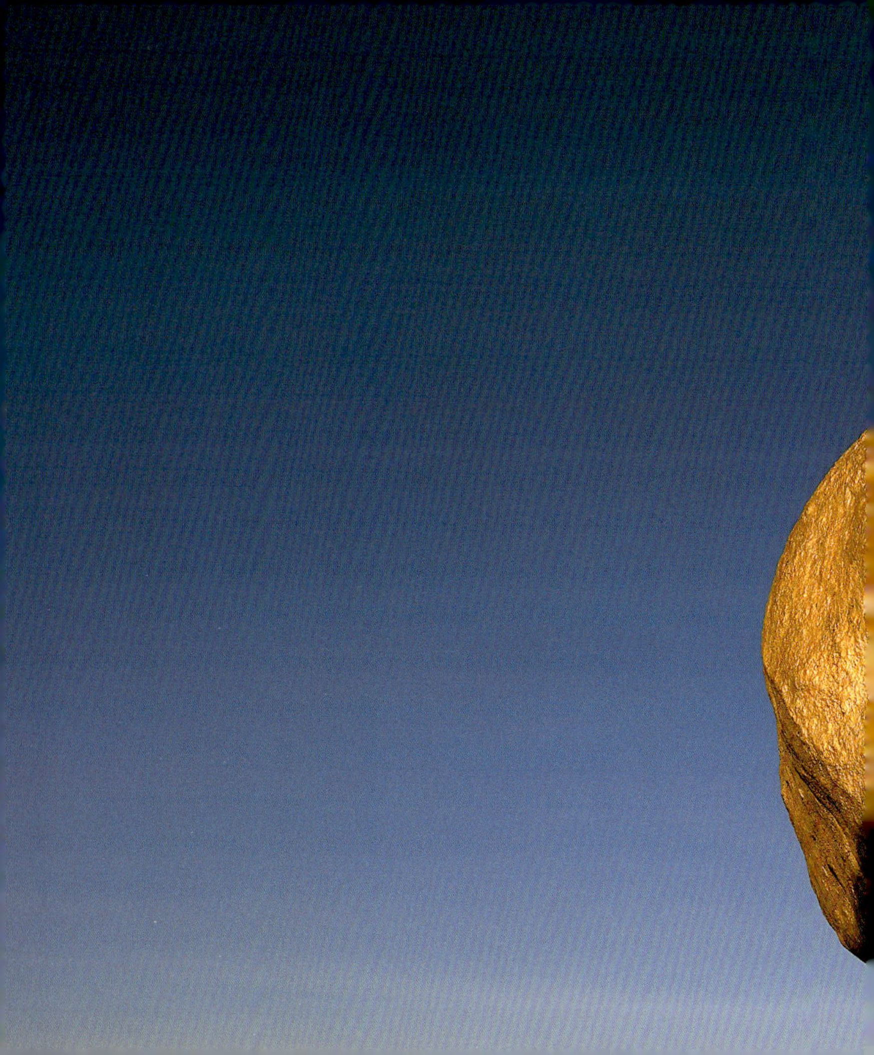

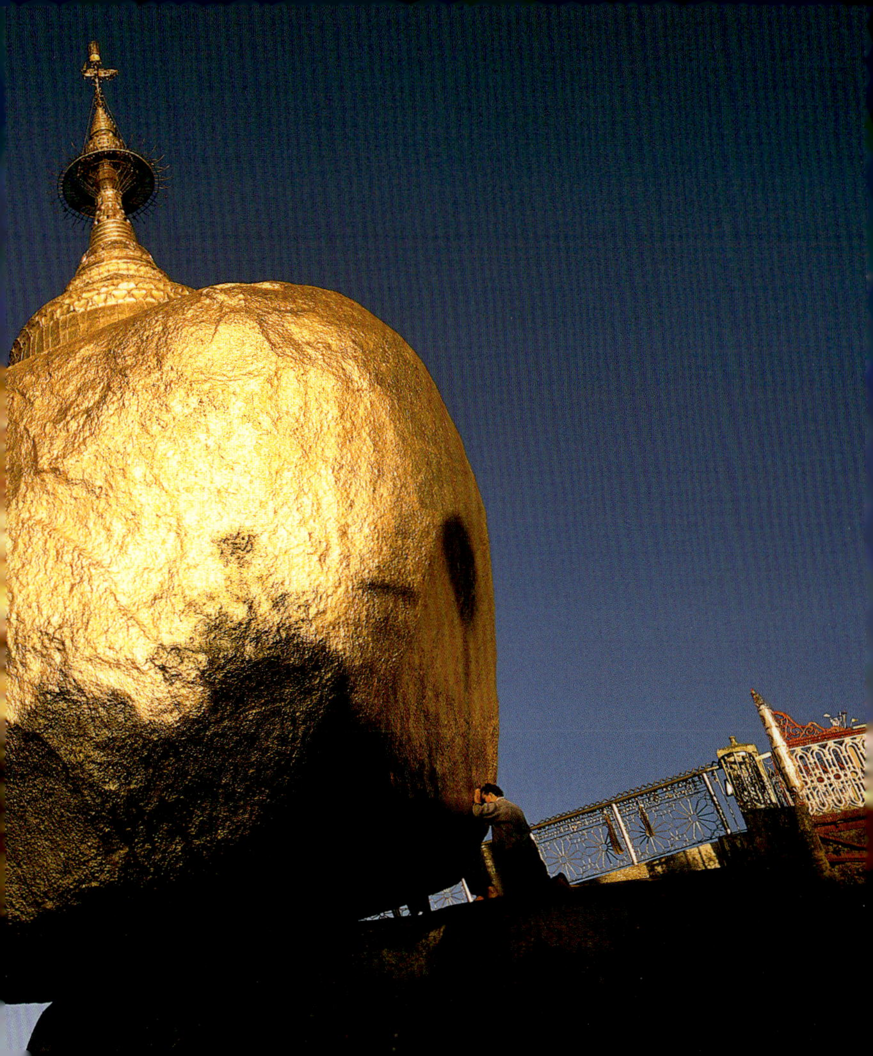

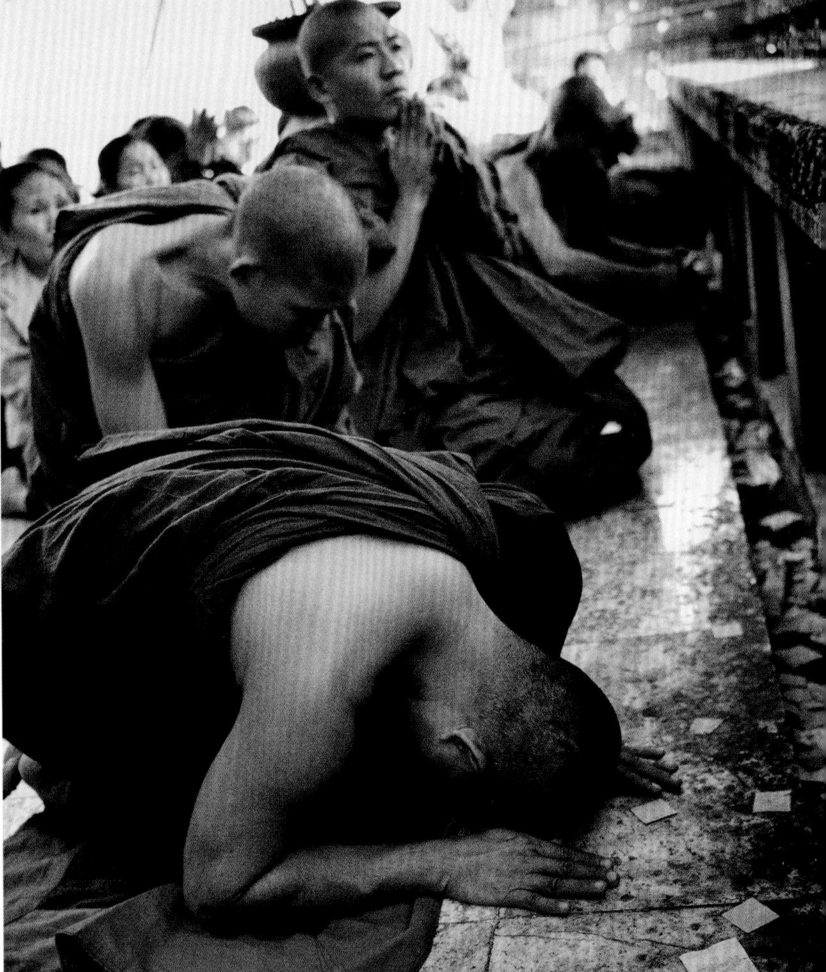

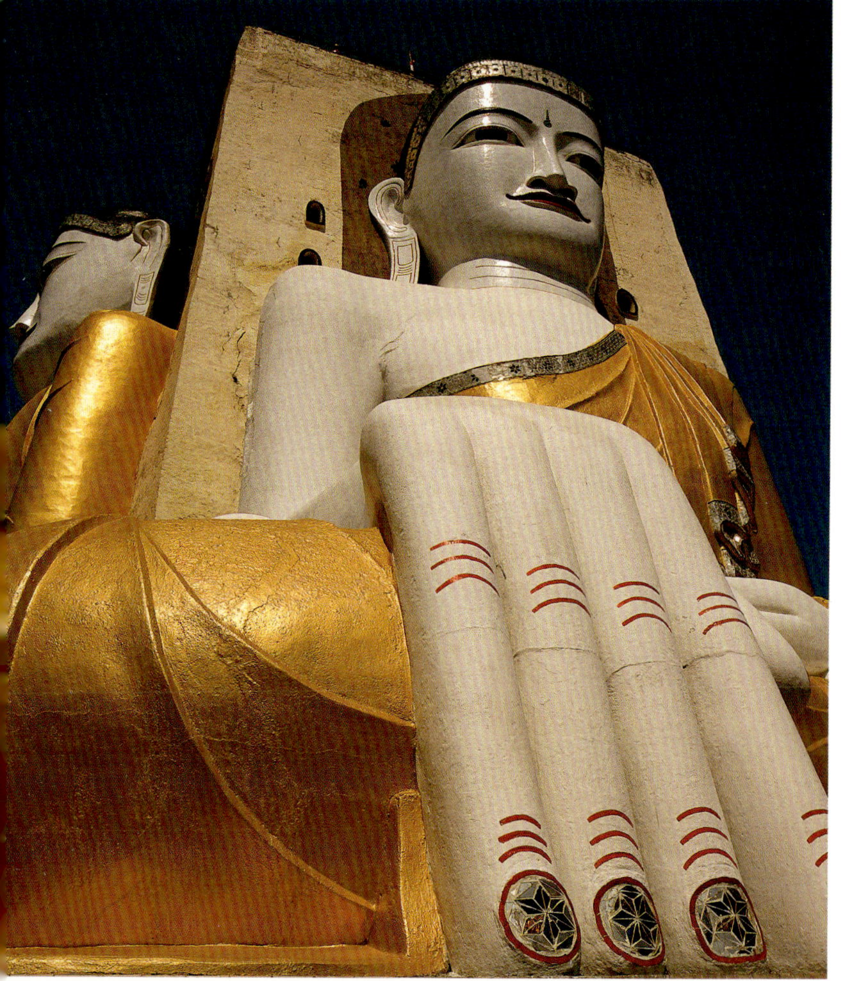

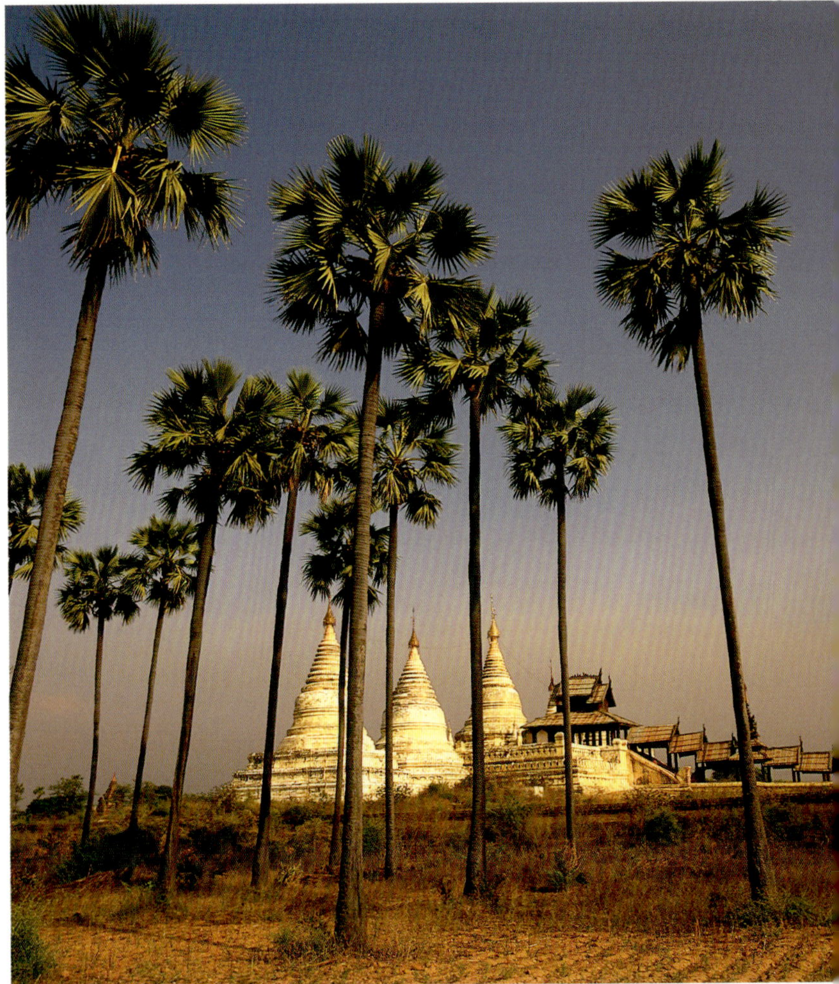

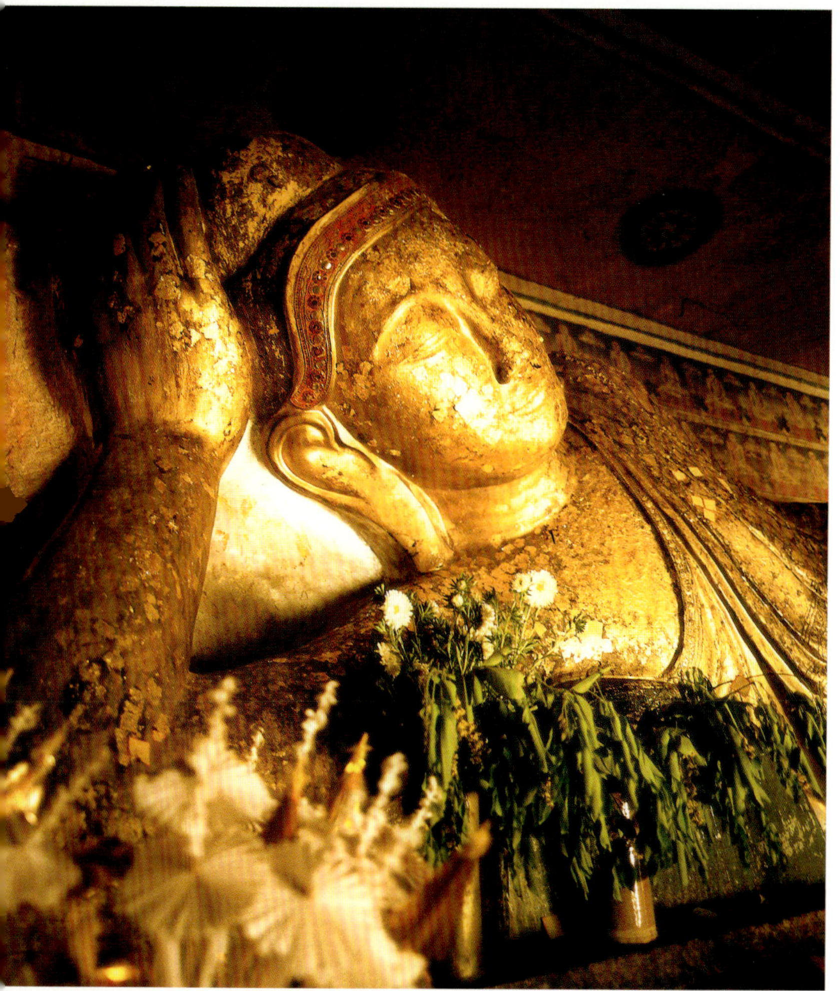

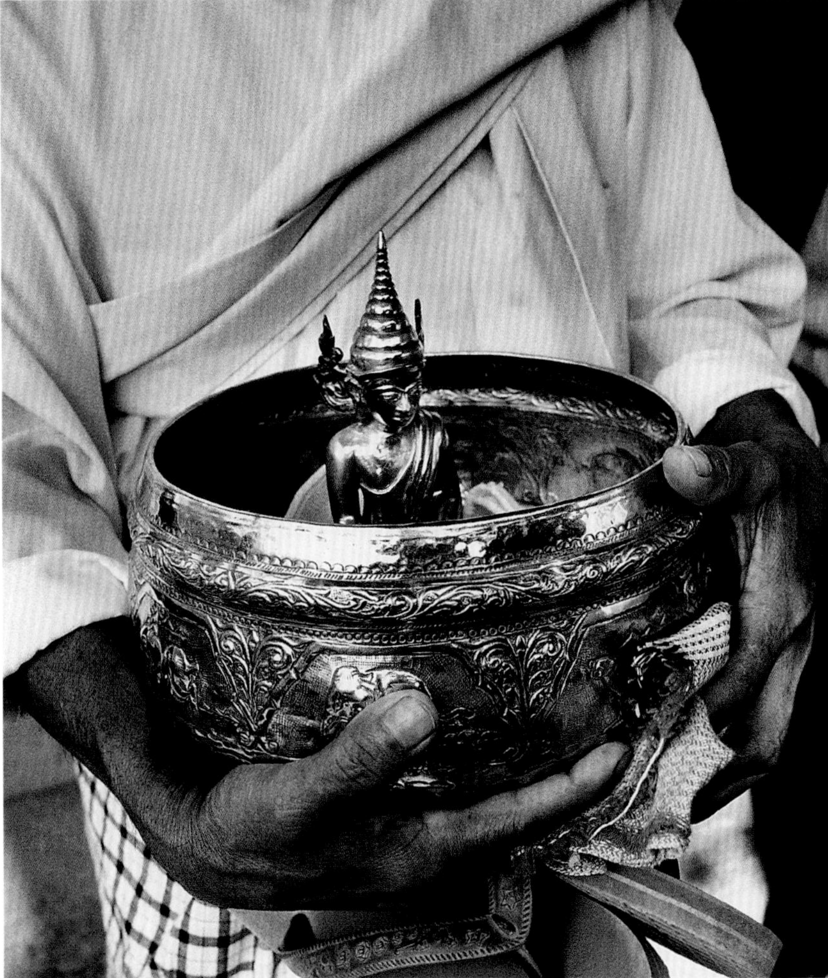

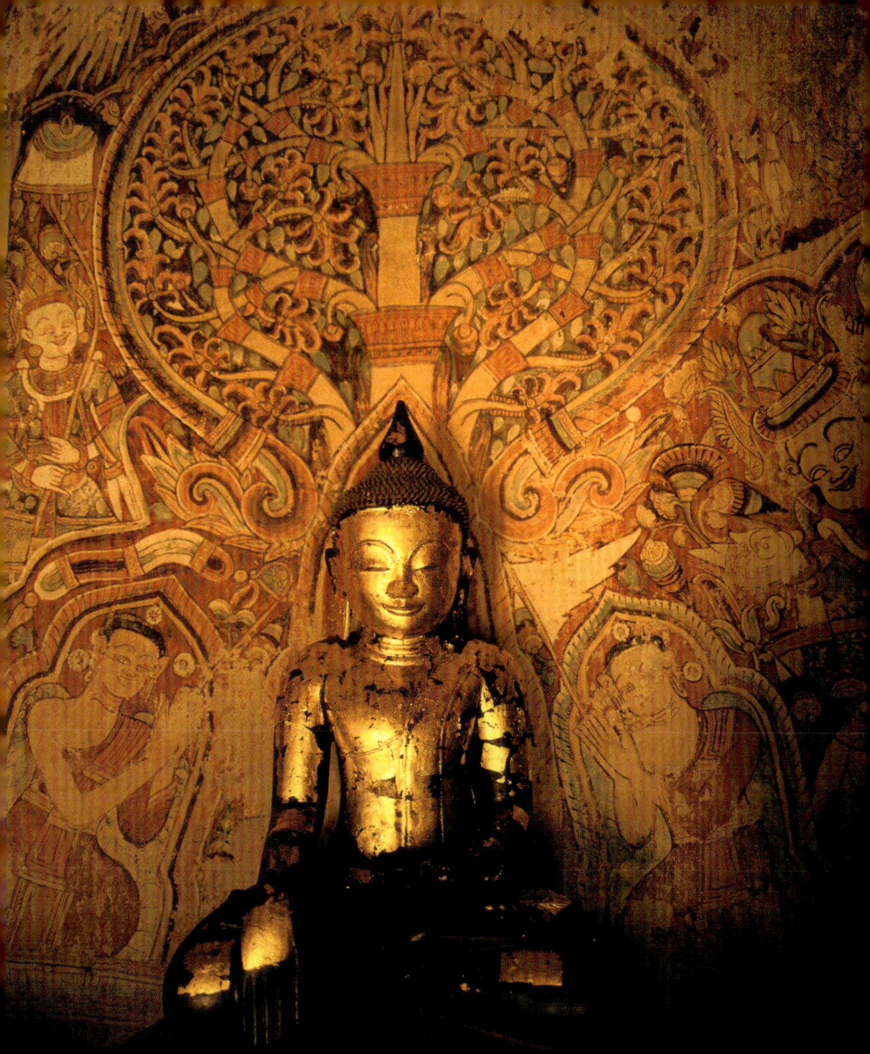

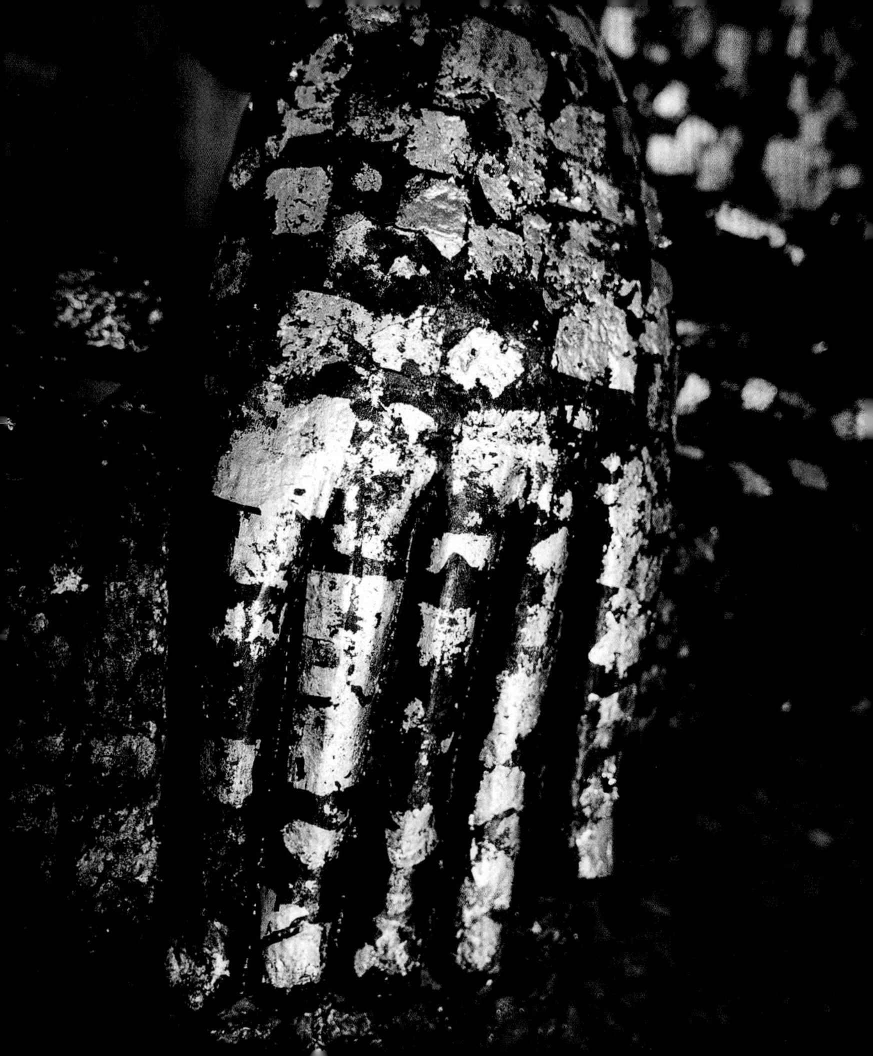

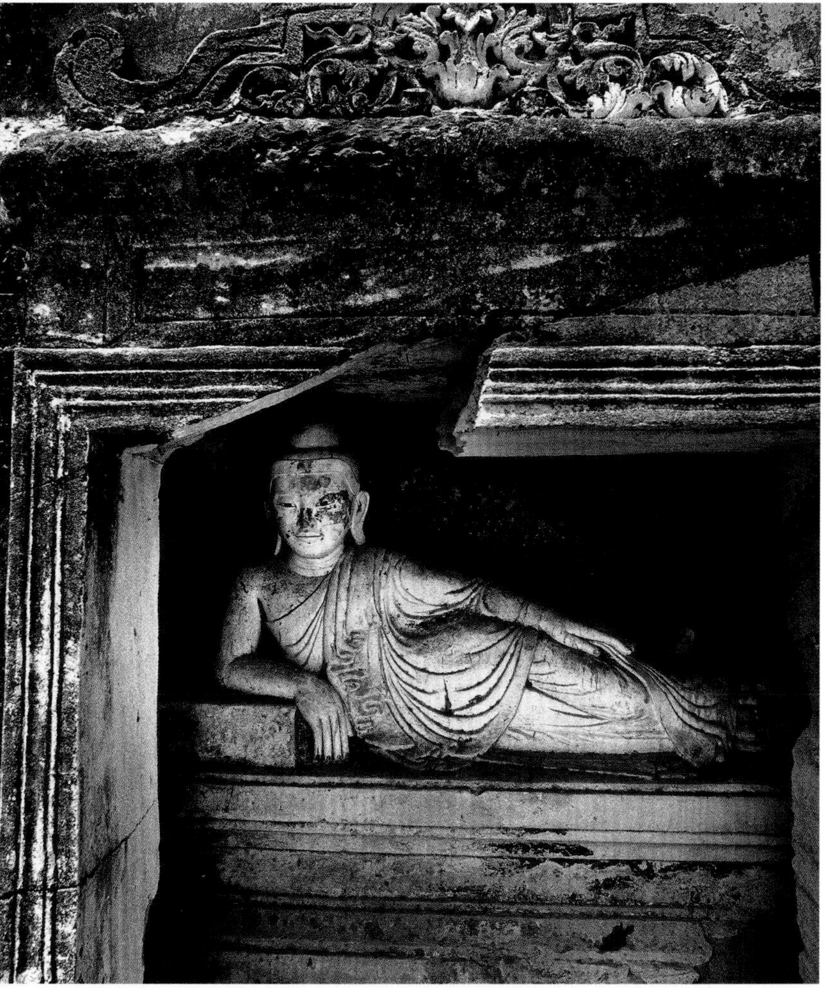

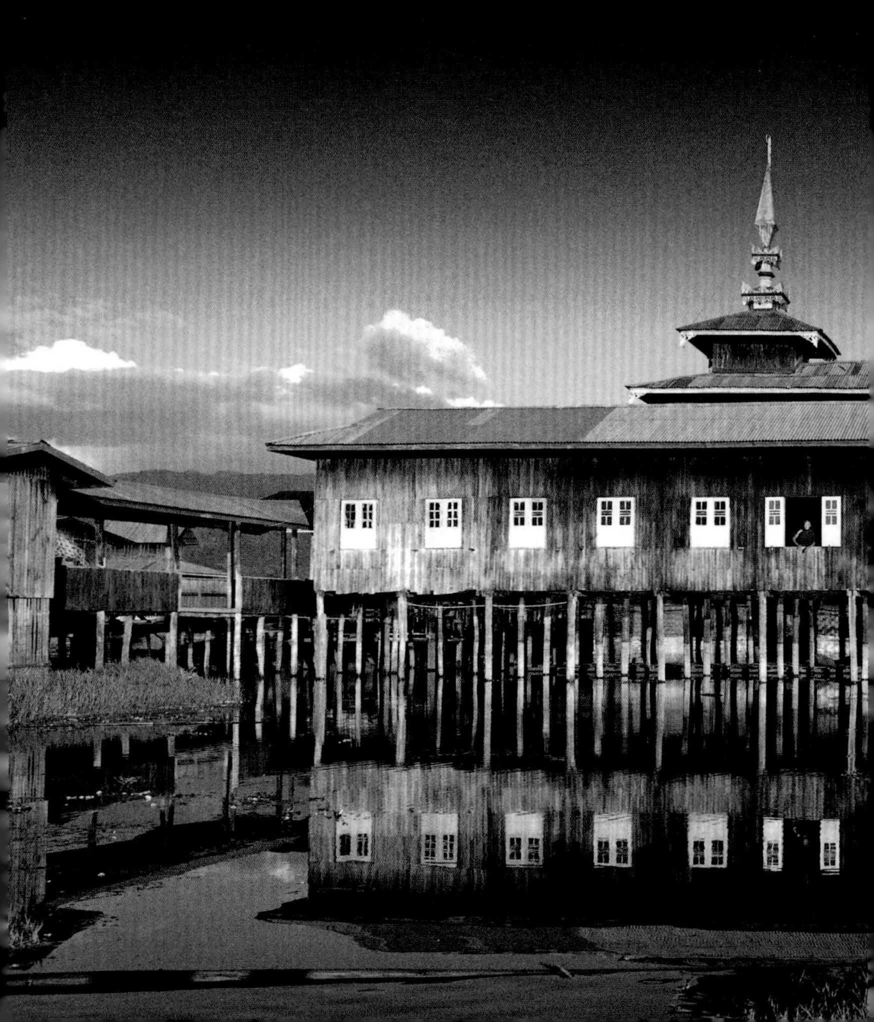

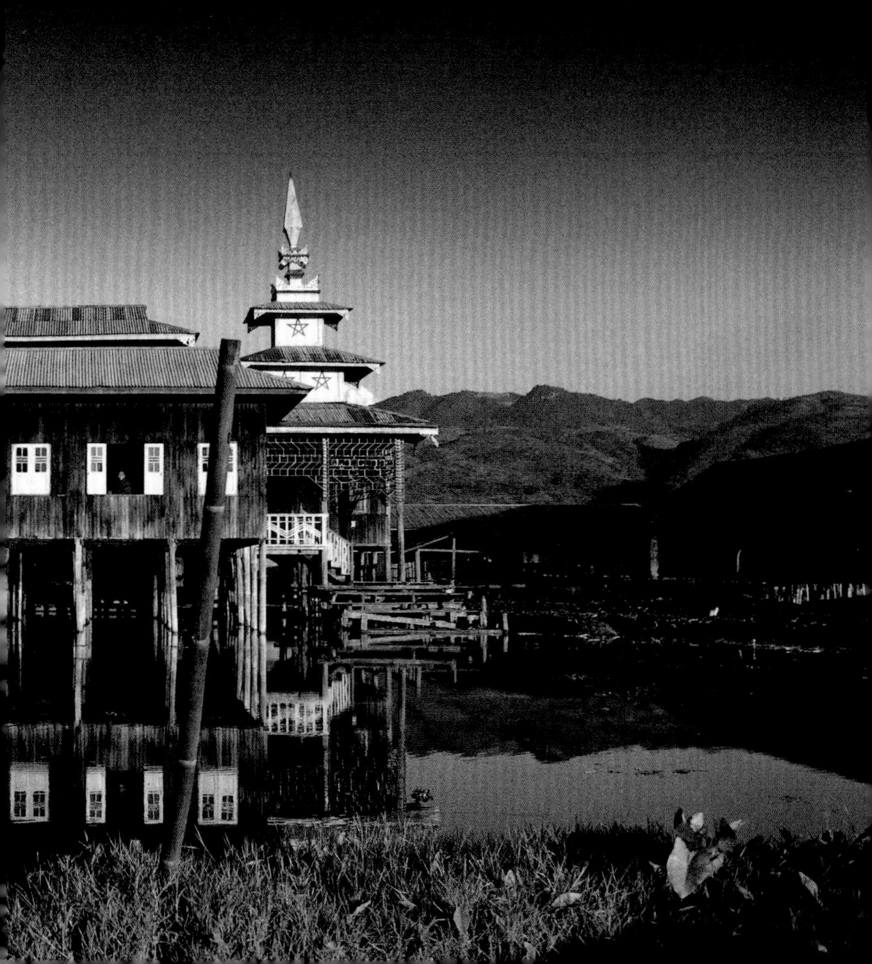

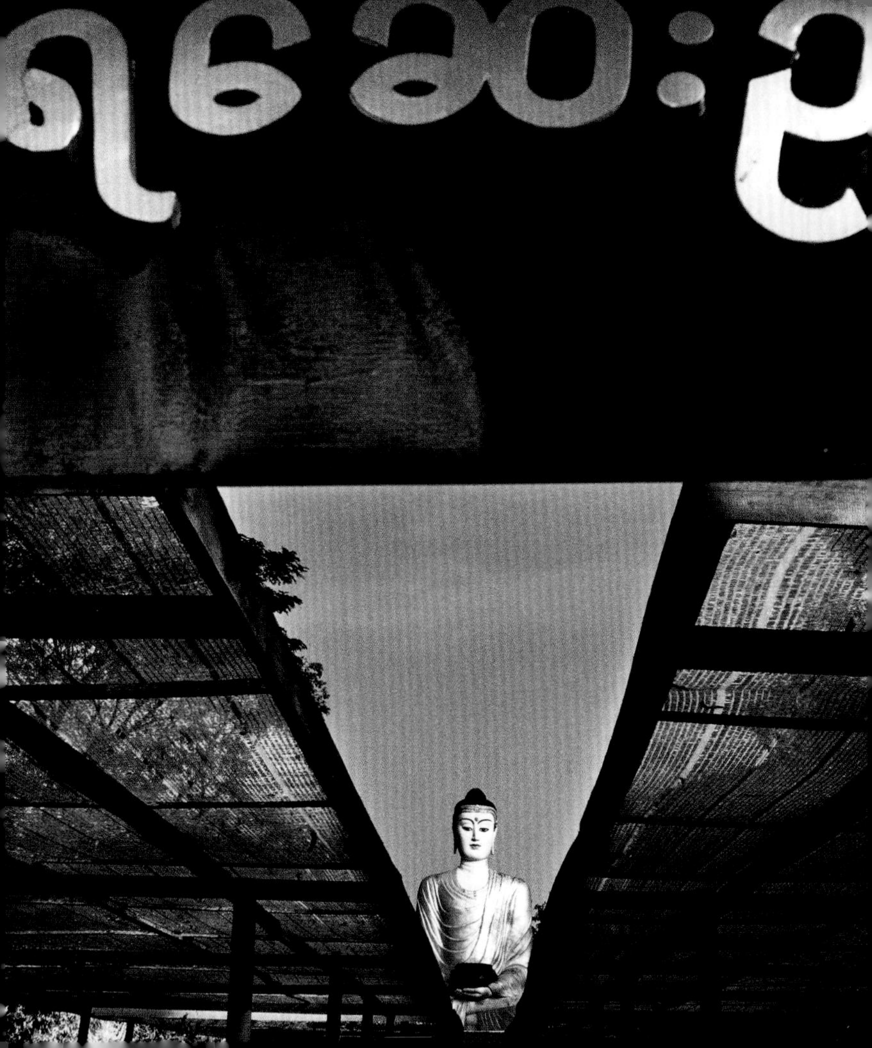

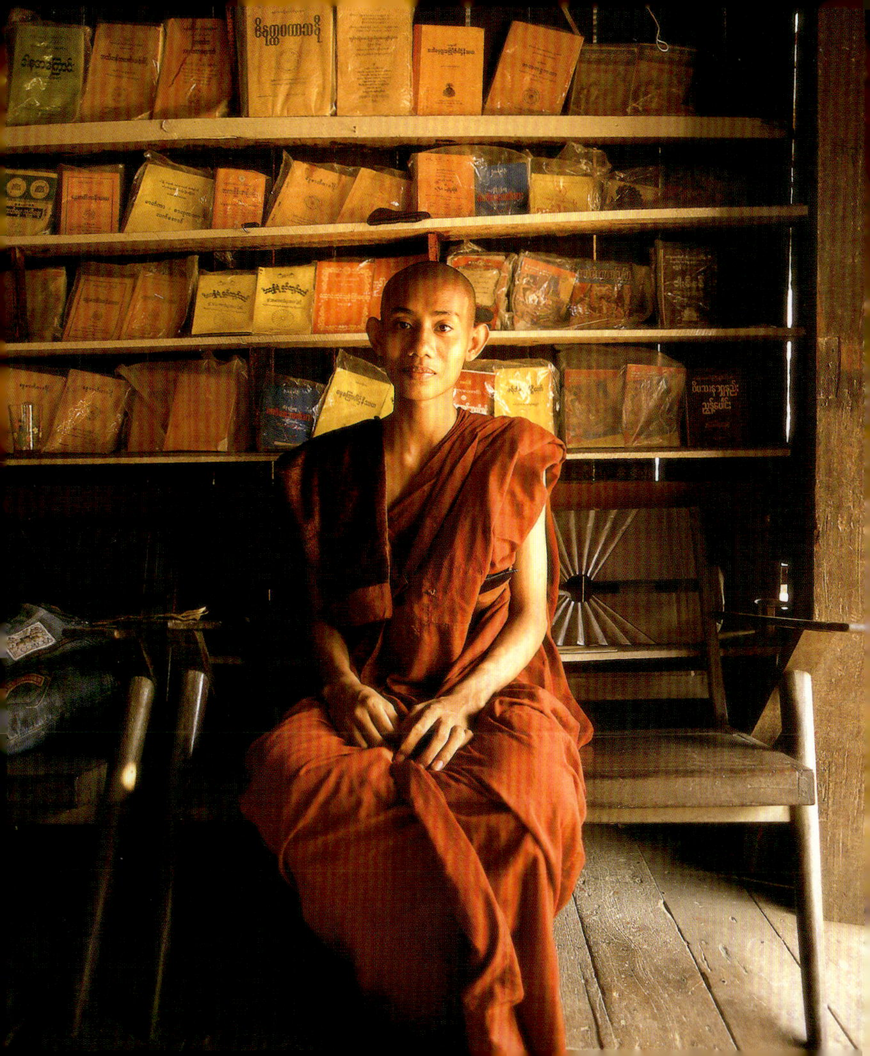

To my parents: Léonie, Simone and Georges, René

My thanks to: Catherine Boretti; Thuzar and Hervé Flejó of Gulliver's Travels, Rangoon; Sekya, our friend from Arakan; Marc Laubscher.

Shambhala Publications, Inc.
Horticultural Hall
300 Massachusetts Avenue
Boston, Massachusetts 02115
www.shambhala.com

9 8 7 6 5 4 3 2 1

Printed in Switzerland
Distributed in the United States by Random House, Inc., and in Canada by Random House of Canada Ltd

Library of Congress Cataloging-in-Publication Data

Grandjean, Jean-Pierre, 1950–
Buddhas of Burma/Jean Pierre-Grandjean.—1st. ed.
p. cm.
ISBN 1-59030-002-5
1. Temples, Buddhist—Burma. 2. Pagodas—Burma.
3. Buddhist art and symbolism—Burma—Pagan.
4. Gautama Buddha—Statues—Burma—Pagan. I. Title
BQ5136.3.B8 G73 2002
294.3'375—dc21
2002021773